W9-BWG-696

LEARN TO TIMBER FRAME

LEARN TO
TIMBER FRAME

CRAFTSMANSHIP • SIMPLICITY • TIMELESS BEAUTY

Will Beemer

Foreword by Jack A. Sobon

Photography by Jared Leeds

Storey Publishing

The mission of Storey Publishing is to serve our customers by publishing practical information that encourages personal independence in harmony with the environment.

Edited by Hannah Fries
Art direction and book design by Jessica Armstrong
Indexed by Samantha Miller

Cover and interior photography by © Jared Leeds Photography, except © 2009 Olaf Protze/Getty Images, 12; Mars Vilaubi, 179, 180; © mcsilvey/iStockphoto.com, 13 (bottom); © nightjar09/iStockphoto.com, 13 (top); © Perry Mastrovito/Design Pics/ Getty Images, 29; Courtesy of SIPschool/www.sipschool.org, 171; © Will Beemer, 10
French carpentry marks chart from *Traité Théorique et Pratique de Charpente*, by Louis Mazerolle, H. Vial Publisher.
Illustrations by © Michael Gellatly

Storey Publishing
210 MASS MoCA Way
North Adams, MA 01247
www.storey.com

Printed in China by R.R. Donnelley
10 9 8 7 6 5 4 3 2 1

Library of Congress Cataloging-in-Publication Data on file

This book is intended to introduce readers to the concepts of timber framing small buildings similar to those shown. The structural engineering formulas and recommendations are meant to be guidelines only and should not be used as the sole factors in determining appropriate design for all conditions. The author and publisher advise that anyone not trained in structural engineering get professional assistance from a licensed engineer before proceeding with construction and follow all applicable state and local building codes. Take proper safety precautions before using potentially dangerous tools and equipment or undertaking potentially dangerous activities. Be alert and vigilant while operating heavy machinery.

ACKNOWLEDGMENTS

Thanks to Jack Sobon for providing the original design and so much inspiration over the years; to Dave Carlon for helping me teach and cut so many of these frames with students; to Tom Barfield for suggesting this book and for his continued support; and to the many students who learned to build these frames and the clients who were brave enough to let them.

In memory of Ed Levin, who taught us the love of timber framing

CONTENTS

FOREWORD *by Jack A. Sobon*

There are pursuits in life that go beyond providing the necessities for our existence, that elevate us above the workaday world, that captivate our imaginations and give us purpose in life. The craft of timber framing is one of those pursuits. It has all the necessary ingredients: a rich historical background that conjures up visions of medieval halls, ornate temples, and pioneer dwellings; a connection to our mother earth (trees are a renewable resource utilized by humans for thousands of years); and a physical, tangible reward for our toil in the form of structures that last for generations. The gratification found in timber framing goes far beyond that of most crafts. We are surrounded by our creative work as it shelters us, enhancing our lives. And what about durability? Timber-framed buildings can certainly last a lifetime, more often centuries. Long after completion, they stand as a testament to our efforts.

This ancient craft, having served humankind for at least 7,000 years, was threatened by the changes brought on by the Industrial Revolution, and became especially endangered in the mid-twentieth century. Old ways and old things were being replaced by the wonders of the new age. Television, plastics, and space travel occupied the minds of most Americans. Plywood, steel, and concrete defined the building industry. It was an era of overcoming and subduing nature, not working with it. As we embraced and focused on new technologies, we were unfortunately leaving behind much knowledge of the old, traditional ways.

By the late '60s, many people were realizing that in our haste to modernize, we had given up some wonderful things. In the back-to-the-land movement that swept our country, timber framing figured prominently. It brought us back to nature, got us involved in building our own homes, and taught people to work together again toward a common good. The formation of the Timber Framer's Guild was a result of that revival. Founded in 1985, it attracted craftsmen and enthusiasts from North America and around the world. Through its outreach, its educational workshops, and its publications, the Guild has fostered the growth of the craft and has assured that timber framing will endure.

Will Beemer has been a leader in the Guild's efforts, especially in its education programs. As an instructor at his Heartwood School and through the Guild's Apprentice Training Program, Will has been perfecting his instruction methods for decades. What follows is clear, concise instruction that will enable timber-frame enthusiasts to get started in the craft. By focusing on a small structure, one can easily learn the concepts, from layout to raising.

Welcome to the world of timber framing!

PREFACE

On a mountaintop in northwestern Connecticut is a collection of 40 or so rustic family camps, little cabins tucked away in the woods by a picturesque lake. Over the years, these families have expanded. As new generations are born and grow up, so grows the need for each group to have its own private space. Kids' cabins and kitchen huts have popped up, as well as storage spaces for kayaks and other sporting and maintenance equipment. A number of these structures share a common origin. It all began in 1988 when one of the mountain residents took a woodworking class at the Heartwood School in western Massachusetts (see Resources, page 181).

Heartwood was founded in 1978 as an "owner-builder" school, teaching the skills needed to build one's own energy-efficient home. My wife, Michele, and I came to Heartwood as instructors in its third year; when the founders left for other things in 1985, we found ourselves running the show. Over the years, Heartwood has expanded to include timber framing and other woodworking skills, using actual projects as teaching tools. One of these projects is a 12 × 16-foot timber frame.

When our visitor from Connecticut came to Heartwood, he saw one of these classic

THE HEARTWOOD SCHOOLHOUSE, *located in the Berkshire Hills of western Massachusetts, was built from trees on the site by the staff and students in 1978–79. The building houses an office, classroom, greenhouse, woodworking shop, library, and dining area.*

frames being built. He realized that this type of building could fill his need for a tool shed and shop on his property and shortly thereafter commissioned one to be built by a Heartwood class. After this frame was completed, he ordered another frame that would become a sleeping cabin near the main house. Over the years, we built 10 more cabins for others on the mountain, each with variations to suit: some were a little larger or smaller, some had lofts or overhangs or different roof pitches. Many of the photos in this book showcase the results.

Over 25 timber frames based on this same design have been built by Heartwood for locations as far away as Argentina and California. The timbers are often precut at the school and shipped for assembly on-site. The attraction of this simple, small timber frame stems from its beauty, functionality, adaptability, expandability, ease of construction, and use of local materials. The carpentry skills and tools required are attainable by most people, and the joinery used is largely the same throughout the many variations on the core design. In this book, we will detail the joinery, illustrate the possible variations, show photos of finished projects, and provide practical guidelines for cutting, raising, and enclosing the frame.

It is encouraging that in recent years more and more people are looking for ways to create shelter with their own hands. As the virtual world of television and the Internet become a larger part of people's lives, the physical world of shelter, food, and nature becomes ever more valued for those who can take the time to appreciate it. The act of making something that has tangible permanence satisfies a basic human need and gives one the opportunity to add personal touches to the design.

These tiny timber frames are excellent first projects for novice builders wanting to start a homestead they can expand. The versatile frames have been built as garden and tool sheds, garages, guest cabins, artist studios, woodworking shops, summer kitchens for large family camps, and additions to larger buildings. The possibilities are limited only by the imagination.

THERE IS A STRONG SENSE OF COMMUNITY AND SATISFACTION *that comes with hand-raising your own timber frame. It's an event to be shared with family and friends: you are creating a structure that will last for generations.*

CHAPTER 1

WHAT IS TIMBER FRAMING?

Timber framing in much of the world can refer to any framing system using wood components, but in North America we use it to mean solid timber (greater than 5 × 5 inches in section) joined together with traditional wooden joinery. It's a type of post-and-beam construction — picture the barn raising in the movie *Witness*.

A Historic Art

Rather than using small framing members (2×4s, 2×8s, etc.) that are closely spaced and simply butt-joined and nailed together, timber framing uses larger pieces spaced farther apart and mortise-and-tenon joinery held together with wooden pins, or pegs. It is the traditional method of framing brought over by the colonists to the New World and can be found worldwide in areas that had abundant timber before the age of sawmills, drying kilns, and mass-produced nails. The same techniques were used to build Asian temples and great wooden ships. The homebuilders in the colonies were often shipwrights, using basic hand tools and minimal material processing (but great skill) to provide shelter. In much of Europe, where centuries-old wooden buildings are still lovingly preserved and valued, carpenters are trained as timber framers and are highly skilled in the techniques shown in this book.

IN THESE CENTURIES-OLD TIMBER FRAMES *in Canterbury, Kent, England, the skill of the builder and the wealth of the owner are reflected in the abundance of carefully crafted timber construction exposed on the outside of the building. This craft is highly valued, and the buildings are preserved accordingly.*

Timber Framing vs. Stick Framing

In North America in the 1830s, settlers migrating west needed a way to build quickly with unskilled labor. The newly built railroad made it possible to ship smaller-dimensioned lumber to the treeless prairie, and the new technologies of sawmills, drying kilns, and mass-produced nails helped promote a new construction system called stick framing. This system relied on the repetitive use of many small pieces of lumber (2×4s, for example) to overcome the scarcity of skilled labor. Now anyone could build a house — and faster, with a smaller crew. Since the framing was nailed together, one didn't need the skills of a joiner. Stick framing became firmly established as the predominant method of light construction after the Great Chicago Fire in 1871, when a large part of the city needed to be rebuilt quickly.

Timber framing, however, remains a viable option, even though it requires more skill. The structures, with their large, open floor plans (no load-bearing interior walls) and exposed timber and joinery, are a joy to make and to live in. If you have a woodlot or access to local sawmills, the materials can be cheaper than buying kiln-dried "sticks" from a lumberyard.

The following chart outlines some of the principal differences between stick framing and timber framing.

A timber frame (top) is composed of large, widely spaced timbers connected with traditional joinery. A stick frame (bottom) is composed of small pieces of closely spaced lumber held together with nails. The frame of a stick-framed building serves as both the structural assembly and the armature for sheathing, insulation, and finish materials; the timber frame requires different enclosure strategies, such as structural insulated panels (see page 170).

DIFFERENCES BETWEEN STICK FRAMING AND TIMBER FRAMING

	STICK FRAMING	TIMBER FRAMING
Size of pieces	Lumber (2×4, 2×6, etc.), planed to a consistent dimension (see Nominal vs. Actual on page 22)	Timber (5×5 and greater), full-size and rough-sawn (not planed) as it comes off a sawmill, usually with some size variation
Spacing	Usually 16 or 24 inches on center to match panelized sheathing materials and insulation	Any, as long as it can accommodate sheathing materials and insulation*
Species	Softwoods, often imported from plantations and mills outside of the region, bought through a lumberyard	Any*, preferably from local forests, produced by a local or on-site sawmill
Moisture content	Kiln-dried	Usually green, not mechanically dried
Connections	Butt joints with nails	Mortise-and-tenon joinery with wooden pins
Bracing for lateral loads	Provided by plywood or OSB sheathing	Diagonal braces or shear walls
Enclosure	Framing covered, with insulation in between	Framing exposed on interior, with insulation layer outside (often structural insulated panels or SIPs)
Skills required	Basic carpentry: simple cuts with circular saw and nailing with a hammer; miscuts are often hidden	Moderate skill: joinery is exposed; irregularities in timber must be accounted for; chisel sharpening
Tools required	Circular saw, hammer	Chisel, mallet for fine work; saws, boring tools for rough-cutting joints
Construction process	Work done on-site with few people	Frame often cut off-site (in shop); erecting the frame often requires a larger crew or crane
Cost	Labor cost is relatively low; materials are equal to timber framing	Labor cost is relatively high

Structural requirements will be considered later, but, simply put, the size of the member (depth and width), the span (length), the species of wood, and the spacing must be suitable for the structural loads (weight) and enclosure methods involved. You can change any of these variables until you find a combination that works, regardless of the framing system used.

Let's look at each of these differences more closely:

SIZE OF PIECES

Timbers are defined as members that are 5 inches by 5 inches or greater; lumber is 2 to 4 inches in its smallest cross-sectional dimension, and boards are 1 inch or less in thickness. This is standard lingo; most of us have a fear of looking dumb at the lumberyard or sawmill, so it's important to have our terminology straight.

SPACING

Over the last century or so, stick framing developed into a highly modular building system based on the standardization of 4 × 8-foot sheet materials — plywood sheathing on the exterior and drywall panels on the interior. Spacing the wall studs and other framing members at 16 or 24 inches on center (measured from the center of one member to the center of the next), ensures equal support for the edges of the panels.

By contrast, traditional timber-frame structures used long, solid-wood planks for flooring and sheathing, and the spacing of the framing was not dictated by the size of the planks, allowing for broad spans between supporting members.

While our timber frame design could be built with lumber, we choose timber mainly because of the aesthetic qualities of the exposed framing and joinery. The insulation and sheathing will wrap outside of the frame rather than bury the frame within the walls and roof.

SPECIES
(and sourcing materials)

Most framing material at the lumberyard is softwood — typically spruce, pine, or fir — that has been distributed through a worldwide commodities network and may come from trees halfway around the world. It has been graded, dried, and planed to produce a consistent product that can be used in mass-produced buildings. Due to the drying, shipping, and storing required, the energy footprint of store-bought lumber is much greater than that of locally milled materials.

Timbers can be of any species and come from your own property, provided they are structurally sound. They can come from a nearby sawmill (of which we have plenty in New England) and thus support the local economy. You can also buy a chainsaw mill or portable bandsaw mill and cut the timber (and lumber and boards) yourself. Hardwoods and softwoods have different characteristics and advantages that will be discussed in the next section. Our timber frame is designed to use eastern white pine (*Pinus strobus*), though other species can be substituted (see page 29).

MOISTURE CONTENT

Freshly cut trees contain a lot of water, and as the wood dries it changes shape, as evidenced by shrinkage, cracking, and perhaps warping. Since store-bought lumber used for stick framing

Softwood and Hardwood

Softwoods generally shrink and move less than hardwoods. Eastern white pine has one of the lowest shrinkage rates and thus ranks at the top of the list of ideal woods for timber framing. If you choose to use mixed species, then usually it's best to frame the larger timbers from softwood and smaller ones (braces, joists, wall girts) from hardwoods.

is kiln-dried and then planed, most of these changes have been shaved away. In the rush to get product to market, however, rapidly grown plantation trees are dried minimally and may still move a bit after construction. Softwood lumber is easy to nail into after drying, which is one reason it's used for framing; hardwoods, although perhaps stronger, are generally much harder and heavier.

Timbers milled locally and recently will be green, so for timber framing it's best to cut the joinery and get the frame erected, then let all the movement take place once the frame is locked together. It's easier to cut joinery in green wood, especially if it is hardwood and you are using hand tools. For wood to air-dry, it takes about a year per inch of thickness, and kiln-drying large pieces is impractical. (There are a couple of radio-frequency, or microwave, kilns in North America that can do the job, but this technique is expensive and works only with certain species.) Using reclaimed timber from old buildings is another strategy for getting "preshrunk" stable timber, but it may need to be re-milled, with a careful eye for hidden embedded metal.

CONNECTIONS

Stick framing evolved in part thanks to the mass production of wire nails. With the multiple redundant pieces used in stick framing, nails were more than sufficient to hold the building together.

Timbers, on the other hand, are too large to nail together, and there are fewer of them, so the joinery connecting them is much more critical. This joinery is usually designed to connect the end of one timber into the side or end of another and often consists of variations of the basic mortise-and-tenon joint.

THE THROUGH MORTISE AND TENON

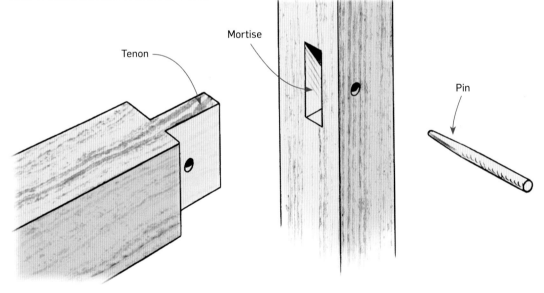

Tenon

Mortise

Pin

THIS SIMPLE TYING JOINT, *in its most basic form, handles moderate loads. It has been used in countless buildings over thousands of years the world over.*

The timbers can literally "frame" the rooms they create. They also provide shelves for displaying items and pegs for hanging your hats.

BRACING FOR LATERAL LOADS

Stick framing usually relies on structural sheathing — plywood or oriented strandboard (OSB) sheets — nailed to the framing every 6 inches or so to provide stiffness and resistance to racking forces from wind and perhaps earthquakes. These sideways forces are known as lateral loads.

Timber framing does not have a stud or rafter every 16 or 24 inches to carry these sheet materials. Instead, diagonal braces provide rigidity, usually running at 45 degrees between a post and a beam, forming the hypotenuse of a right triangle. Shear walls (explained later) may also be required by some building codes in areas with high lateral load potential from seismic or hurricane events.

ENCLOSURE

With stick framing, the regular spacing of framing members provides bays of equal width to accept standardized batts of insulation, as well as support for exterior sheathing that in turn carries siding and roofing. These same framing members are then covered up on the inside with gypsum drywall or other materials (after wiring and plumbing runs are installed), so the frame is completely concealed.

For timber frames to be enclosed in the same manner, a redundant stick-framed system would need to be built outside of the timber frame (if you want to see the timbers exposed on the interior). Because the timber frame is carrying the loads, however, this light frame, or curtain wall, would not need all the components (such as headers) that a structural stick-framed system would have. This external light frame is common, but the popularity of timber framing really exploded with the advent of the structural insulated panel, or SIP. These panels are made of rigid foam insulation sandwiched between layers of plywood or OSB and can be built to span areas as great as 8 × 24 feet. They are attached to the outside of timbers with long screws. SIPs have made it unnecessary to build another light frame outside of the timber frame.

SKILLS REQUIRED

Both stick framing and timber framing require carpentry skills such as reading plans and a tape measure and being able to cut a straight line with a saw. A stick framer, though, is usually working with standardized materials of uniform dimensions and following established patterns and methods for assembly. This is why there are rarely stick framing plans included with a set of construction drawings; once the carpenter knows the dimensions of the building and locations of doors, windows, and interior walls, he or she can frame the building using the chosen on-center spacing.

Timber framing, however, requires more of the skills of a woodworker. Wood as it comes out of the sawmill is green and somewhat irregular. Designing, locating, cutting, and assembling joinery in such material must still result in a structure that stands plumb, level, and square. This requires patience, attention, understanding, and specialized skills, including the ability to visualize the finished structure while the raw timber is sitting on the sawhorses. Since the timbers and joinery will usually remain exposed, greater care must be taken since errors won't be covered up. A job well done, however, results in that much greater satisfaction.

TOOLS REQUIRED

Stick building may only require a saw, square, hammer, tape measure, chalk line, level, and pencil. Power tools and pneumatic nailers make the job go faster, but not necessarily better.

Timber framing requires additional tools, mainly to execute the joinery. Timbers are large and heavy and may require a cart or many hands to be moved. Because of irregularities, framing squares and combination squares are useful for keeping joinery true to reference planes in the building. Tenons can be cut with saws or even with an axe, but mortises are generally harder to

WHILE SOME TIMBER FRAMING TOOLS *will require a significant financial investment, others, such as commanders and mallets, can be made from materials at hand.*

cut. They require a boring tool, such as a drill with large bit, an antique boring machine (beam drill), or modern electric chain mortiser. Mallets and timber framing chisels are the primary hand tools for cutting, and even finishing, joints that have been roughly cut with power tools. Mallets may be used for driving pins as well, with heavier versions called commanders (also *beetles* or *persuaders*) used to drive timber assemblies together.

CONSTRUCTION PROCESS

Most stick-built houses (excepting manufactured kits) are still cut and assembled on-site, with floors built on foundations that will serve as the platforms for ever-higher walls and, finally, the roof. Weather, access, and distance from the builder's home can affect the speed at which the project is completed.

Timber framing is, in a sense, a kit or "pre-manufactured" structure. You can cut the frame in a barn, shop, or garage away from the site, protected from the weather, and close to home. Then you take the pieces of the frame to the site and erect it in a matter of hours. You need an area to store the timbers (covered, ideally) and to work

them, and then a truck or trailer to transport them to the site. Of course, if the woodlot sourcing the timber is the same as your building site, it would make sense to work them there.

Both stick-framed walls and timber-framed bents are typically assembled flat on the deck and then are tilted up into place. Since timbers are heavier, you usually need more people to raise a timber assembly, or even to install individual rafters. Cranes, forklifts, or other mechanized equipment are used on big jobs.

COST

In terms of the amount of framing material used, similar-sized structures usually use the same volume of wood whether they are stick-built or timber-framed. Wood volume is measured in board feet; one board foot (BF) is the volume of a board 12 inches by 12 inches by 1 inch thick. If you are comparing lumberyard framing materials at $1/bf to local sawmill timbers at $0.75/bf, it's cheaper to do timber framing. Buying timbers from across the country, however, would end up being more expensive. If you're paying for labor, timber framing is usually more expensive because of the skill involved. But if you're doing

the work yourself, labor cost is not a factor. However, it will usually take longer to build a timber frame (though you'll have that pride of accomplishment).

Other factors affecting cost are the enclosure and insulation system and the level of finish. Often people who have a nice timber frame upgrade the rest of the systems to match. Using local sawmill lumber and boards for sheathing, siding, paneling, cabinets, and flooring can produce significant savings. Finally, timber frames have a lower life-cycle cost: the frame lasts longer (sometimes hundreds of years), since it is protected inside an insulated envelope and is often well-maintained.

All in all, if you're providing your own labor and buying local materials, a timber frame can cost less than a stick-built structure you build yourself with lumberyard materials. The timber frame built with local materials is also environmentally friendly and has a strength and beauty valued by its owner. Of course, if all you want is an uninsulated storage hut in the garden and plan to pay for labor, it's pretty hard to beat the cost of a stick-built prefab shed from a big-box store. But that's not why you picked up this book.

CHAPTER 2

GETTING STARTED

For millennia, people have timber framed without the benefit of building codes or standardized materials. It's only in the last century or so that the building "industry" has become so prescriptive that a narrow set of guidelines — recipes, if you will — usually dictates how to build a house. For those who wish to build with traditional methods, such as timber framing with local materials, a more thorough understanding of the materials and techniques of the craft is necessary. The species, sizes, and shapes of the building materials are guided by the builder's vision and often go beyond what is specified by the building code.

Using Ungraded Native Timber

The timber frame in this book assumes the use of "native" timber, from trees locally harvested and sawn (or hand-hewn) to size either on-site or at a nearby sawmill. Actually, it's unlikely you could even find timbers at a conventional lumberyard; the largest timber usually stocked is a 6×6 or 6×8, and our timber frame uses 7×7s to 7×10s or larger. We also recommend using timber that is green and ungraded. As mentioned in chapter 1, using green timber is less a problem if you use a species with low shrinkage rates and get the frame up quickly. You generally don't want to mill timbers from logs and then let them sit for years to air-dry; they may twist enough to require re-milling. If you have to wait, it would be better to peel the logs (to keep out bugs) and then mill the timbers square later, just before cutting joinery and raising.

The frame can also be designed (as ours has) to minimize the effects of shrinkage. Since wood shrinks much less lengthwise than across its width, posts should run as long as possible — from sills to plates (the whole height of the building) —

with intermediate beams joining into them. Compare this to platform framing (the standard design of stick-frame houses), in which a beam sits on a short post with another post sitting on top of it to continue upward. When this beam shrinks across its width, thus shortening the vertical height of the beam, the entire building drops a bit. Conversely, if the beam joins into a continuous post, the beam can shrink but the post will stay the same length.

BUILDING CODES

Using ungraded timber is an issue that brings us to building inspectors and codes. The building code is a set of prescriptive minimum requirements, enforced by the local building authority, to ensure the safety and performance of buildings. The building authority usually is the city or municipal building department, and code compliance is assessed and verified by a building inspector. While most building codes are modeled after state or regional codes, such as the widely used International Residential Code (IRC), the local building code is the final word on what is allowed in its jurisdiction. Specific code requirements can vary by city, county, or state.

For wood-frame construction of houses, most codes only cover conventional stick framing, not timber framing, which continues to be a small,

Start Small

The frames shown in this book are small enough to give you a useful but manageable first project for learning timber framing. It's easy to underestimate the amount of time it takes to complete a building project: the frame is just the beginning, then it must be enclosed and finished. We always advise owner-builders to build small and add on later, and the frames shown here have that adaptability. With the skills you'll learn — and an adaptable design — you'll probably find yourself adding on with the help of your kids and grandkids down the line.

specialized part of the construction world. For stick framing, the code includes tables that show the allowable spans for graded lumber. The stamp you'll find on every piece of lumber in the lumberyard indicates its strength as determined by an inspector when it came out of the mill. That grade, such as Select Structural, No. 1, or No. 2, tells the builder what line to go to in the table to see what span and load that piece can carry. These tables only cover lumber, not timbers.

Timbers from your own woodlot or a local sawmill will not be graded, since graders usually work only at large mills that mass-produce framing lumber. While the IRC doesn't have a clause about using native (ungraded) lumber, many states that have a significant timber resource have their own amendments that allow the use of it for structural purposes in one- and two-family dwellings. It is up to the building designer to make sure the timber used is the proper size for the conditions, and it's up to the sawyer and builder to make sure the timber is of adequate quality (no rot, large knots, or other defects). Much of this is based on experience: designers have formulas to size timbers in lieu

HOW WOOD SHRINKS

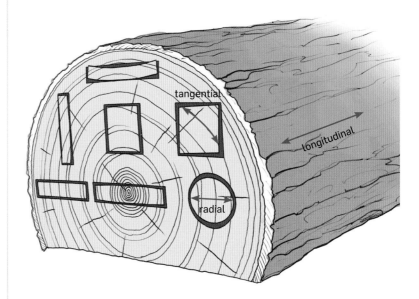

WOOD CHANGES SHAPE AS THE WOOD CELLS DRY OUT. *Sections of wood with growth rings of varying lengths will not distort uniformly, since the rings with more wood cells will shrink more than the rings with fewer. Tangential shrinkage (along the growth rings) is greater than radial shrinkage (across the rings). Wood shrinks least longitudinally (along the timber length).*

Nominal vs. Actual

The size of lumber and timbers may be specified with nominal or actual dimensions (generally, if there are no inch marks after a dimension, it's nominal). This means its actual dimensions may vary. For example, a nominal 6×6 at the lumberyard may be actually 5½ × 5½ inches, because ½ inch has been planed off after drying the original 6×6. We will use nominal dimensions throughout most of this book. However, since you will be dealing with sawmill (not lumberyard) timbers for this project, the actual dimension should be fairly close to nominal; say, within ¼ inch. A good sawyer can produce green timber within ⅛ inch of nominal and very square; get recommendations from local timber framers about whom they use.

of the code tables, and good sawyers will know, if told what the timber is for, how to select the proper quality of logs.

Following the IRC, most state and local codes don't require a building permit for one-story storage and accessory buildings under a certain size. In some areas the maximum footprint is 120 square feet or less, but in many others it is 200 square feet (our standard 12 × 16-foot frame is 192 square feet). So if no permit is required, the building inspector may not even be involved in your project to enforce the code, although you should still follow the code where applicable. And be aware that other features of your project may trigger permit requirements, such as the addition of plumbing, the type of foundation, siting, etc. Any plans to live in a building — classifying it as habitable — will almost surely get the attention of the building department and require a permit.

Local zoning may not even allow accessory or detached buildings, no matter what size. While building codes dictate the materials and methods to make the building safe and perform well, zoning specifies what the allowed *uses* of a building may be, and stipulate minimum requirements such as lot size, road frontage, and perhaps even orientation and appearance.

The building department can be your best friend or your worst enemy. Get to know the folks there and find out what you can do by showing them the design of the project and explaining that you want to timber frame it using native material. At best, they may tell

FOR AN INVESTMENT OF A FEW THOUSAND DOLLARS *a small bandsaw mill like this can easily produce all the timbers for this frame plus boards for flooring, paneling, and sheathing. Portable mills can also be hired to come to your site.*

you to go ahead and no permit is required. At worst, they may require you to hire a structural engineer to review and stamp the plans, and perhaps require that you get the timber graded. You could buy your timber from mills that grade timber (few and far between). Alternatively, you can hire a grader to come and grade the timber on your site.

The building department may also suggest (or require) the type of foundation to use. For accessory buildings without plumbing, foundation requirements are often minimal. Many building inspectors in the northeastern United States are familiar enough with timber framing to recognize its inherent strength and can intuitively judge the adequacy of a frame design. This is especially true in rural areas, where they have had to deal with generations of farmers and homesteaders with barns and outbuildings. Building inspectors who are unfamiliar with timber framing may default to requiring an engineer or architect to approve the design, since it is not covered in the code.

UNDERSTANDING LUMBER GRADE

Native lumber provisions in the building code will likely specify that ungraded timbers be sized as if they are No. 2 grade, the lowest grade allowed for structural purposes. The sizes of the timbers used in this book's project have been calculated using that grade. Most timber framers learn to visually grade timbers themselves (even though they aren't officially certified to do so) by using the "measurement of characteristics" described in the rules book of the regional grading agency. For example, the species eastern white pine is handled by the Northeastern Lumber Manufacturers Association (NeLMA; see Resources). Its grading book, available as a free download on the association's website, shows how to measure things like knot diameter, checks and splits, slope of grain, and other limiting characteristics that determine whether a given piece is No. 1 or No. 2. (To be certified as a grader by NeLMA involves an extensive course and is available only to employees of NeLMA or mills that are members of NeLMA.) NeLMA is the agency to contact if you need to hire a grader for most species in the northeastern United States; other agencies govern southern and western species.

The timber frames shown in this book are designed for using No. 2 eastern white pine in the moderately snowy climate of southwestern New England, where we have a snow load of 50 pounds per square foot. Your conditions may vary. Next, we'll look at how a frame is structurally engineered, to highlight where you may need to consider possible changes to the designs. Mainly this will be in the sizing of rafters and plates to reflect varying snow loads.

Is It Registered?

One more caveat about buying timber: some state codes (Massachusetts, for example) allow the use of ungraded native lumber but require that it be produced by a state-registered mill. I suspect this is mostly a bureaucratic tool to keep track of who is selling what (and who should be paying taxes), and most small mills around here have paid the nominal fee to register. Homeowners using their own wood may be exempt from this requirement in some locales, but anyone can register as a mill, even if all they're using is an axe to process timber.

Timber-Frame Engineering 101

Any structure is subject to forces, called loads, exerted on it by a number of causes and must adequately resist them in order to keep standing. The forces are transferred through the structure and down to the ground via *stresses* in the components; these stresses are compression (materials pressing together), tension (materials pulling apart), and shear (materials sliding relative to one another), and often occur in combination in a given component. The structure resists these forces in three ways: through strong pieces (the timbers), strong connections (the joinery), and rigidity (diagonal bracing or structural sheathing).

Rigidity, used to resist lateral loads such as wind and earth-quakes, is accomplished by diagonally bracing with as large a brace as practical. A triangle is an inherently stable structure. We all know from looking at old timber-framed barns that are still standing that diagonal braces work. However, there is always some "play" in the building, depending on the accuracy and tight fit of the brace joinery. While diagonal braces are more than sufficient for our small timber frames, for larger buildings engineers might specify that structural panels, such as plywood, oriented strandboard (OSB), or structural insulated panels (SIPs), be fastened to the framing to create "shear walls" for additional stability. Indeed, this would be required in seismic areas such as California, and the diagonal timber braces would be redundant.

When the frame is loaded laterally, such as when a strong wind is blowing against one side of the building, some braces will be in compression and some in tension, depending on their placement. Since it is best to consider joinery as working only in compression (and we don't want to rely on the pin alone to resist tension forces), we assume the braces in compression will provide resistance to sideways pressure. We can't predict from which side the lateral loading will come, so we generally want at least two opposing braces in each plane (longitudinal and transverse sections) of the frame.

Most of your concern (and your building inspector's) involves the proper sizing of pieces, especially frame members that span horizontally. These are beams, as opposed to posts (vertical members) and braces. Why do we concern ourselves with the size of beams more than posts or braces? This has to do with the nature of wood. Wood is anisotropic, which means that it behaves differently depending on the

KINDS OF STRESS

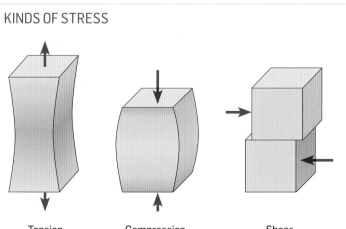

Tension   Compression   Shear

BEAM UNDER A BENDING LOAD

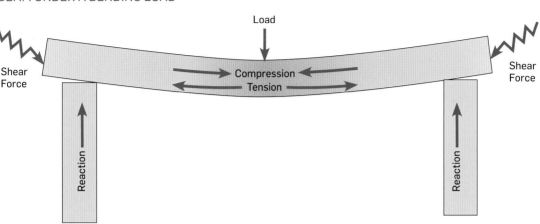

direction of forces applied to it. This is due to the grain or orientation of the wood cells. These cells are much longer parallel to the long direction of tree growth, and wood can resist stresses parallel to the grain much better than stresses perpendicular to the grain.

Imagine grabbing a wood pencil at both ends and trying to pull it apart (tension parallel to the grain) — can't be done. Likewise, you couldn't push on both ends of a blunt pencil and crush it (compression parallel to the grain), although it might buckle (a separate problem). Posts (and braces, when there is lateral load on the frame) are usually the frame members in compression, and posts are typically 7×7 or larger, mainly to fit the joinery. This is more than large enough to handle any

compressive loads. Buckling doesn't concern us in timber framing unless the posts are excessively tall and slender (like a 20-foot-tall 4×4). In our frame, the main member in tension is the tie beam (see page 83) that resists the outward thrust of the roof, and it is the end joint that would fail long before the beam itself pulls apart. Hence the wedged dovetail joint, which is one of the strongest tension joints in timber framing.

When forces are applied *perpendicular* to the grain, like with a floor joist supporting a piano or a rafter carrying a snow load, the wood beam behaves differently. The beam deflects as it transfers the load out to the supports at its ends. This behavior is *bending*. As the beam bends, the top is trying get shorter (in compression) and the bottom is

trying to get longer (in tension), while the longitudinal planes of wood fibers are trying to slide past each other (in shear) to accommodate this.

To size such beams — including sills, joists, rafters, plates, and tie beams — a designer must complete three steps:

1. Determine the loads.

2. Determine the species of wood.

3. Match the size of the timber (depth and width) with the span (unsupported timber length) and on-center spacing using formulas or tables (if available).

As mentioned earlier, I have done this work to provide a

framing system that is appropriate for our area. It's beyond the scope of this book to go through the structural formulas, but we can look at each of these steps in more detail to see where different conditions in your area may affect the component sizes.

Further research can help you determine new sizes for timbers, if required. Jack Sobon's *Build a Classic Timber-Framed House* has an excellent section on structural design. If you need a professional to review your design, structural engineers can be found through the Timber Frame Engineering Council (see Resources).

LOADS

Loads include the weight of everything that is applying force to the structure. These include four types:

Dead load is the weight of the building materials: timbers, flooring, roofing, insulation, drywall, etc. We've used a dead load of 10 pounds per square foot (psf) to size our beams, which assumes conventional flooring, roofing, siding, etc. If we take the area of the floor or a wall, for example, and multiply it by 10 psf, that gives us the approximate weight of that area. This psf figure is a good average for anywhere; the weight of building materials doesn't

change from place to place (at least on this planet). However, if you wanted to put 4 inches of concrete (at 150 psf) on the floor joists, or a living roof with 12 inches of earth (at 120 psf) on the rafters, then the framing components would need to be resized to carry the additional weight. Engineers use tables that provide the weights of materials to add up the different layers and come up with an exact figure.

Live load is the weight that people and furnishings add to the building. The building code stipulates 40 psf for living areas (including kitchens and appliances), 30 psf for sleeping

Joinery: Tension and Compression

Little data is available on the strength of timber-frame connections (joinery); much is intuitive and based on historical precedents, although testing is being done to determine the strength of timber joints with wooden pins. If one avoids tension joinery — which can rely too much on the pins to take the stress — and avoids making multiple connections in the same part of a timber, the major loads can be carried by the large surfaces where the timbers meet rather than by the pins or the mortises and tenons within the joints.

Such is the case in our frame design. The only tension joint in the frame is the wedged dovetail on the tie beams, and the pin does little work there. Actually, the pins are used mainly to draw the joints together, hold them together during raising, and act as springs (through *drawboring*) to keep the joinery tight as the frame shrinks. You could remove all of the pins from the frame after it is erected and it wouldn't fall down. But why do that? The pins provide great places to hang things and should not be cut off flush, except on the exterior or where they would be a hazard.

areas, and 20 psf for storage areas. We have used 40 psf to size our ground floor joists and 30 psf for loft joists. This might be overkill for a storage shed, unless you park a tractor in it. On the other hand, a stack of green oak firewood 8 feet high could weigh over 300 psf.

Snow load is the number most likely to vary in your design. We have sized the rafters to carry 50 psf of snow (standard for western Massachusetts). By comparison, this figure would be 25 psf on Cape Cod. In the Rocky Mountains, snow loads can be over 200 psf. You will need to consult your local building department or the Internet to find your specific snow load. This is the "ground" or flat roof snow load; there are other adjustments to account for roof slope, drifting and sliding snow, and more, but these factors shouldn't affect the designs shown here.

Wind loads vary widely but are generally not a concern with a well-braced frame in most locales. Once the building is enclosed, the combined dead load will probably exceed the lateral loads imposed on a windward wall and roof, especially if the building is in the woods. Exceptions may occur

in high-wind areas such as sea-coasts, and in these areas it is just as critical to anchor your structure well to a good foundation. Consult with a local builder or the building department for advice. Structures that have roofs closed in but walls open, such as pavilions and gazebos (or your frame before you put your doors and windows in), can be subject to significant uplift during high winds.

The designs in this book assume uniformly distributed loads, not extremely heavy loads concentrated in the middle of a span. There are other formulas for that and other conditions (such as cantilevered beams) that require different calculations. Consult a design professional if you need to check the beam sizing for such cases.

LOADS ON A STRUCTURE

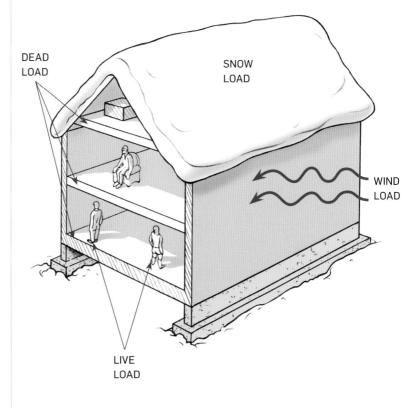

DEAD LOAD

SNOW LOAD

WIND LOAD

LIVE LOAD

SPECIES OF WOOD

Different woods have different strength characteristics, but just about any wood can be used to timber frame. Wood strength is represented by *design values*, data determined through testing that is published in various sources to be used in formulas to size the beams. As mentioned, our timber frame is designed to use No. 2 eastern white pine (EWP); equivalent species would be spruce, red pine, and balsam fir. EWP is relatively weak (though cedar is slightly weaker), so you can substitute stronger woods, such as hemlock, most hardwoods, or most western softwoods (like Douglas fir), in your frame without changing sizes. We choose EWP for its many other shining virtues: it shrinks the least of any species (except cedar), it is lightweight and easy to work with hand tools, and it is plentiful in our area in large sizes and lengths.

These are the three main design values we look for when sizing beams:

• **Fiber stress in bending,** or Fb, is a measure of the strength of the species. For No. 2 EWP, the Fb is 575 psi.

• **Shear parallel to the grain,** or Fv, tells us (for example) how much we can notch the ends

EASTERN WHITE PINE IS ONE OF OUR FAVORITE WOODS *for timber framing. It's light, easy to work with hand or power tools, plentiful in large-sized logs, and shrinks the least of almost any wood.*

of our floor joists. This value is 125 psi for No. 2 EWP.

• **Modulus of elasticity,** or E, tells us the stiffness of the species, which rules the design of floor joists so they don't bounce; it's less of a concern with rafters. For No. 2 EWP, this value is 900,000 psi.

Note: Any species of wood that has the same (or greater) design values can be substituted in the frame designs in this book without changing sizes, providing the loads are the same or less. (See page 178 for comparative design values.)

SIZING THE BEAMS

Once we have determined the loads and the species we are going to use, we plug those numbers into formulas, along with the actual cross-sectional size of the timber (say, 7 × 9 inches), the span of the timber (its unsupported length), and its spacing from similar timbers on both sides sharing equivalent loads. Joists in the middle of the floor take more load than end joists, so we take the worst-case scenario and size members according to the ones taking the greatest load.

Ordering and Storing Timbers

Once you have the timber list (also called scantlings) you can order your timbers. It's best to have the trees cut and milled in the winter; there will be less dirt in the logs if pulled from the woods over snow. Also, EWP and some other species are prone to blue stain, a harmless fungus that grows in the sapwood once the juices start flowing in the spring. This is a purely cosmetic defect; it doesn't affect the wood structurally.

Loggers will cut trees somewhat longer (6 to 8 inches) than nominal length, which is usually given in 2-foot increments (8 feet, 10 feet, 12 feet, etc.). This gives you a little bit of play when it comes time to lay out the joinery. You may want to avoid knots or other defects that can make cutting joinery more difficult, even if they don't affect the timber grade. If you are worried about the quality of timber, order 2 feet longer than you need to ensure even more

options during layout. In other words, if you need a timber 12 feet long, order a 14-footer. Most sawmills can cut timber up to 16 feet, but if you need longer lengths the price will start to go up, and some sawmills have trouble going longer than 24 feet. Here in western Massachusetts we have mills that cut up to 40-foot lengths. With portable sawmills the length is limited only by the number of bed extensions or the ingenuity of the operator.

STORING TIMBERS

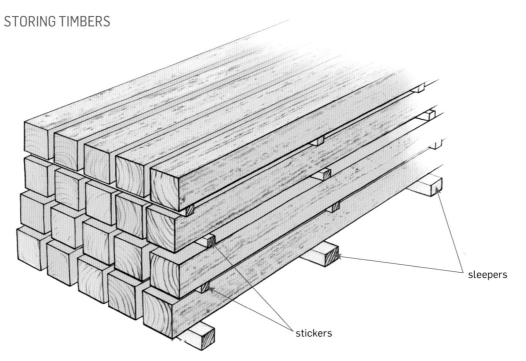

sleepers

stickers

Use 1-inch stickers to separate layers of timbers and sleepers to keep them up off the ground.

Large timbers (greater than 5×5) should be specified as boxed heart, which means that the pith or center of the tree is completely enclosed in the timber. This helps to minimize distortion and checking (splitting that occurs while drying). The sawyer gets a large timber from the center of the log and then cuts minor timbers and boards from the outer pieces (or cants). In large western species, such as Douglas fir, it's possible to get even the biggest timber "free of heart center" or FOHC, and this pretty much eliminates any checking, since checks occur from the pith out to the nearest face. In eastern North America, though, we don't have many trees big enough to saw FOHC.

Once your timbers are delivered, stack them so they have plenty of air circulation around each piece. This can be done by placing sleepers — 4×4 or 6×6 timbers laid on the ground — about 4 feet apart and in a level plane. Then stack layers of timbers of similar depth with about 1 inch between each timber and 1-inch-square boards, or stickers, separating each layer. You can order some low-grade extra timbers for sleepers from the sawyer, who may also saw you some stickers; alternatively, you can rip some strips of wood on a table saw. Label the timbers with their size and length on the end grain, using a crayon or felt marker. Cover the stack of timbers (corrugated metal

roofing works well), but leave the ends open for air circulation.

Think about how you will get into the stack to pull timbers out as you need them for layout and cutting. Professional shops have forklifts; you may be working alone with nothing but a timber cart, or with a friend. It's generally most efficient to work on all similar timbers at the same time, so get all the braces out and done, then move on to joists, then rafters, etc. The big advantage of the square rule technique that we will explain in chapter 3 is that you can work each piece independent of the others.

Should You Order Extra Timbers?

Ordering extra timbers is generally a good idea to cover you in case you make a mistake or a timber has unacceptable defects, although there may be no rejects from a good sawyer. Order an extra brace, joist, and rafter piece, since these are smaller and relatively inexpensive. If you have the capability to re-saw material to a smaller size if necessary, order one or two extra of your longest and largest timber, and consider what you can use them for if you don't need them. If you cut a number of these frames, eventually you'll have an inventory of extras so that you only have to order what you need for each frame.

CHAPTER 3

LAYOUT SYSTEMS

Layout describes the process of locating and marking the joinery that will connect timbers together in the frame. In stick framing with dimensional lumber, this is fairly straightforward, since all lumber is planed to consistent size. But in timber framing with rough sawmill material, the timbers vary somewhat in dimension and squareness. The key to layout is to account for these variations to produce a structure that stands plumb, level, and square; is of perfect outside dimensions; and has all surfaces flush that will accept flooring, siding, and roofing.

Layout Basics

The surfaces and outside dimensions of the structure are called reference planes, and are indicated on the plans as the faces from which dimensions are taken. The outsides of exterior walls and the tops of floor joists and rafters are reference planes. Most timbers in the frame will have one or two reference faces in a reference plane. For example, each of the two adjacent outside faces of a corner post is a reference face because each lies on the reference plane of an exterior wall. (A centerline within a timber could also indicate a reference plane, such as in a round post in the interior of a structure, since it has no flat faces.) Interior posts and beams don't have a surface on the exterior of the building, so a convention must be adopted to determine the reference plane. Traditionally, this might be a compass point (the north side, for instance), or the side of the member facing the nearest exterior bent, or the side facing the center aisle, or the centerline.

There are four layout systems in general use today in timber framing: square rule, scribe rule, mapping, and mill rule (*rule* here means a system of measurement, not a set of laws). We will focus on square rule in this book, but first we'll look at each system in reverse order to see how each can be used to find the overall lengths of pieces, our first step in layout. This step can be done at your desk or workbench before you ever start moving timbers off the stack.

Look at the floor plan for our basic 12 × 16-foot frame (comprised of sills and joists). Dimensions are given to the exterior (reference) faces of the sills; the other reference face would be the top of the floor system, since we want the flooring to lie flat. (The underside of the sills may need to be shimmed to account for irregularities, depending on the foundation system.)

FLOOR PLAN

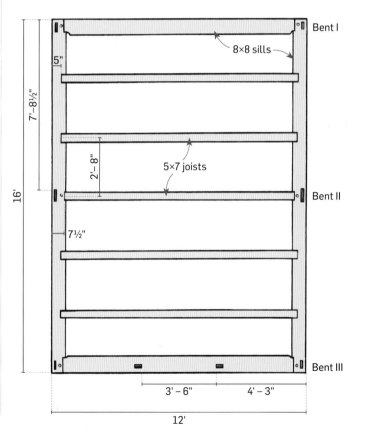

Bent I

8×8 sills

5"

7'–8½"

2'–8"

5×7 joists

16'

Bent II

7½"

Bent III

3' – 6" 4' – 3"

12'

Let's consider the length of the short sills, which have tenons, and the long sills, which have mortises. Since the ends of the long sills are cut to the exterior dimensions, the length is easy to determine: 16 feet. The short sill has a tenon going into the long sill, and the shoulder of the tenoned joint bears against the inside face of the long sill. The shoulder-to-shoulder length of tenoned pieces is the critical dimension that will finally determine the size of the building. We don't care so much (yet) about tenon length; they could be a little short and not affect the overall dimensions of the structure.

MILL RULE

In mill rule, timbers are planed on all four sides to a perfectly square section of consistent dimension. For example, an 8×8 coming off the sawmill at $8\frac{1}{8} \times 7\frac{3}{4}$ inches is planed down to a perfect $7\frac{1}{2} \times 7\frac{1}{2}$ inches. This planing, or *sizing*, can't be done efficiently by hand, even with a portable power planer. It generally requires buying your timbers from a mill that has a timber sizer or shipping your timbers to such a mill for planing. While many large timber framing shops have their own sizers and use this system of layout for its simplicity, it's generally not an economical option for owner-builders who don't live near a mill with a sizer.

In our example, using mill rule, the shoulder-to-shoulder length of the short sills would be 12 feet (the width of the building) minus 15 inches ($7\frac{1}{2}$ inches times two, the two long sills' combined actual width), for a total of 10 feet 9 inches. Then we would add the tenon lengths. Here we need to stress a very important point: the shoulder-to-shoulder length controls the overall dimensions of the building. If we add the tenon lengths to get an overall length of timber, we could make a math mistake — that would

be trouble. Instead, we just lay the tape measure on the timber to locate shoulder-to-shoulder length and make sure we have enough extra for 3-, 4-, or 5-inch tenons, however long they need to be. With mill rule, because all timbers are a consistent dimension, similar timbers with the same theoretical length, such as joists, braces, and rafters, are interchangeable.

MAPPING

With mapping, we take the variation in width of one timber and compensate by adding or subtracting length on the timber joining it (remember, the timbers haven't been planed to a consistent dimension). For example, if one of our long sills is $7\frac{3}{4}$ inches at the end where it meets the short sill, and the other long sill is $8\frac{1}{8}$ inches where it joins to the other end of the short sill, the shoulder-to-shoulder length of the short sill becomes 12 feet less $7\frac{3}{4}$ inches less $8\frac{1}{8}$ inches, or 10 feet $8\frac{1}{8}$ inches. Because the long sills could vary in width from end to end, the other short sill's length could be different, so in mapping, similar pieces are *not* interchangeable.

Mapping is sometimes referred to as "distance scribing," since in scribe rule (described next) you transfer

TIMBER TIP

It pays to find a good sawyer who supplies other timber framers in your area and go to the mill to measure some of their product for squareness before hiring them. Good sawyers can consistently provide timber within $\frac{1}{16}$ inch of square and $\frac{1}{8}$ inch of nominal dimension.

the variations in one timber directly to the mating piece placed above or below it. You do the same thing in mapping, but not directly. Instead, you measure the variations and carry them (in your head or a notepad) over to the mate. Mapping is much too cumbersome and confusing a process when done on an entire frame, but is useful to know if you make a mistake and can compensate for it in the layout of the mating piece.

Because mill rule does not require compensating for variations, and mapping is used (by us) only in an emergency, we don't consider them true layout "systems" like scribe rule and square rule.

SCRIBE RULE

Scribe rule is used most often for very irregular timbers and logs: round, twisted, bowed, and forked tree shapes — anything you couldn't use a framing square on. Using scribe rule, all of these irregularities are just as easy as to work with as square stock. In this system, each uncut timber is laid out horizontally but above one another in the position they will take in the final frame assembly, usually over a drawing on the floor. The entire assembly is carefully leveled, and using plumb and level as the universal reference planes, irregularities at the joints are transferred from one piece to another by hand and eye, using plumb bobs on strings, dividers, or other devices. No numerical measuring is required other than during the layout of the original floor drawing. Indeed, scribing was developed before literacy and numeracy were prevalent in the trades.

Scribing requires the most skill of all the methods described here but often produces the best fits; many timber framers use it even with very straight and square stock. However, pieces are not interchangeable, and this method requires a large shop floor or other area to perform layout. There is also much handling of timber, since you need all of the pieces in an assembly present and accounted for in order to lay them out.

In the case of our sills, we would need to place the two long sills parallel to each other exactly 12 feet apart (measured to their outside faces), set the short sills on top of them, make sure the whole setup is level, and then transfer the joinery intersections visually without ever calculating a shoulder-to-shoulder length. Scribe rule layout would require a book unto itself to fully explain, and there is very little written about the system other than what we suggest in the Resources section.

SQUARE RULE

We consider square rule to be the layout method of choice, both for pros and novices of the craft. It is simple to learn and doesn't require a lot of shop space (each piece can be worked on independently), and similar pieces are interchangeable. Square rule developed in early America, where builders had access to large trees that they could hew or saw reasonably square without concern for waste. (In Europe, smaller, crooked trees were all that was available, and every inch of diameter was needed, so scribe rule was — and still is — used extensively.)

With timber surfaces true and square enough to be used as references, square rule assumes that a smaller perfect timber lies within. This perfect timber can usually share two reference surfaces of the larger timber; often you will find at least two adjacent square faces on a timber from a reputable sawmill. The joinery on the opposite (non-reference) faces can then be laid out to the inner surfaces of the perfect timber. This is done by reducing the size of the timber at the joint. Since the sizing reductions are laid out at uniform distances from reference faces (or in the case of a bowed timber, to a chalk line snapped parallel to them), they may vary in depth according to how much larger any actual given timber might be than its perfect-timber-within. Sometimes a rough timber may be so out of square that the perfect timber can't share any of its surfaces; in this case, centerlines or other reference planes must be laid out square to each other on the timber ends and connected down the length with chalk lines.

We'll consider the joinery layout in more detail later, but for now let's return to considering the length of the short sills. With square rule, we will look at all of our timber upon delivery and see how much variation there is from nominal. If the greatest variation is ¼ inch above or below nominal, we can say that we are going to frame our perfect timbers to ½ inch under nominal. If the variation is more than ½ inch under nominal (some nominal 8-inch timbers actually measure 7⅜ inches,

for example), then you may need to frame to 1 inch under nominal and get a different sawyer next time. Using the ½-inch benchmark, we then reduce each end of the long sills to 7½ inches at the joint, and the shoulder-to-shoulder length of the short sills will be 12 feet less 15 inches, or 10 feet 9 inches. We'll do the same at the other end of the building, so both short sills will be the same length (and interchangeable,

barring other differences such as mortises for door posts in one sill and not the other).

As you can see in the drawing labeled Square Rule Reduction, when you lay out the long sill, you will mark a housing (a shallow cavity to receive the end of the adjoining timber) on its inner (non-reference) face, 7½ inches from the outer (reference) face, and the length of that housing along the grain will also be 7½ inches. When you cut the

SQUARE RULE REDUCTION

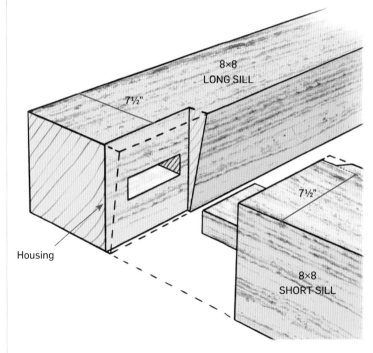

The housing is laid out 7½ inches from the outer reference face of the long sill. On an out-of-square timber, this reduction essentially exposes the face of the "perfect timber within." The width of the tenoned sill is also reduced to 7½ inches a short distance back from the shoulder so that the mating pieces are flush.

mating short (tenoned) sill, you will know to reduce its width to 7½ inches for a short distance back from the shoulder to clear any unreduced width in the long sill. You never need to see or measure the mating pieces to lay out or cut the joinery.

In summary, traditional square rule joinery is laid out parallel to, and the same distance from, a reference face. Thus, reference faces will be flush to one another; even interior braces will be flush to one side of their posts and beams, not centered. This feature, along with the use of housings on most pieces, distinguishes square rule from the other systems. The advantages are the interchangeability of pieces and the fact that joinery can be laid out without seeing the mating piece (maybe it hasn't even been sawn yet). The disadvantage is that the reductions that create the smaller perfect timber require extra work, both in creating the housing and reducing the tenoned piece.

We'll focus on the square rule method in subsequent procedures. As you practice layout and get familiar with the system, it will become intuitive and less mysterious. We'll explain the finer points of layout as we get into the details of the frame and clarify the system. Your

TYPICAL SQUARE RULE LAYOUT

IN SQUARE RULE, *all joinery is laid out parallel to, and the same distance from, a reference face. Reference faces are therefore flush to one another, as the interior brace shown here is flush to one side of the post, not centered. A red triangle indicates the arris (see page 56), the edge shared by two reference faces.*

final objective is to have a frame that is plumb, level, square, and straight. A chalk line can be snapped on a curvy timber to establish a straight plane, and spirit levels can find plumb and level. A framing square can be placed against references faces to transfer points and planes around a timber. Many of these skills come with experience but are fundamental to becoming a good builder. The projects described here will help you get there.

CHAPTER 4

TOOLS

Timber framing tools can be grouped in pairs: there are layout tools and cutting tools; there are hand tools and power tools; and there are carpentry tools that can usually be bought at the local hardware store and specialized timber framing tools that you need to order or even make yourself. What you buy or need will depend somewhat on how many frames you plan to build and whether you want to become a professional. But I suggest two rules to control your acquisition of tools: buy the best you can afford, and don't buy a tool until you need it. A quality tool will not only last longer; it will generally be more accurate and have higher resale value than a lower-quality tool, and it will be a pleasure to use.

Tools for Layout

Layout tools can be further grouped into measuring and marking tools, and they are all hand (not electric) tools, with the exception of laser levels, which might be used in scribe rule and site layout.

MEASURING

Tape measure: Use a standard 16- or 25-foot tape, depending on the length of your timbers; a 50- or 100-foot tape is useful for measuring diagonals when squaring up frame assemblies prior to raising. If you want to have only one tape measure, make it a 25-footer. If you're working alone on the timbers, get a tape with a wider blade (1 inch) that will make it easier to hook on the end of the timber. Use the tape measure to measure lengths and locate joinery along the timber; once it comes to laying out individual joints, put the tape away and move to a rigid tool (like a square) for more accuracy.

Framing square: The modern version of this ancient tool has 16-inch and 24-inch legs that are 1½ inches wide (the *tongue*) and 2 inches wide (the blade or *body*) respectively. The outside corner where they come together is the *heel*. Not coincidentally, our mortise widths and tenon thicknesses are all 1½ inches and laid out 1½ inches from the reference face. (Tenons are usually about ¼ the thickness of the timber, so we would go up to 2-inch tenons

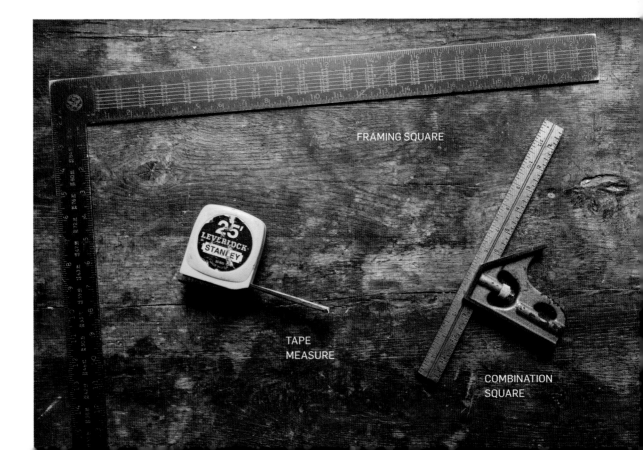

FRAMING SQUARE

TAPE MEASURE

COMBINATION SQUARE

if we were using 8-inch timbers, 3-inch tenons for 12-inch timbers, etc.) This makes the framing square very useful for laying out joinery, and indeed this was its main purpose when it was invented in timber framing's heyday in the 1800s.

The framing square is also used to check the squareness and twist (if any) of the timber and to transfer marks and lines around the timber, sometimes in combination with other tools. If the timber is out of square, the framing square becomes indispensable for finding reference planes. The 1½-inch tongue makes it easy to check the width of mortises and to lay out holes for the pins (wooden pegs or trunnels), which are almost always 1½ or 2 inches off the joint's shoulder.

Framing squares are typically aluminum, steel, or stainless steel. Aluminum squares are lightweight and don't rust, but they are not as durable as steel squares, which unfortunately can rust and become unreadable. If you want the best, buy a stainless steel square, though for one frame it might be overkill.

Combination square: This tool has fallen out of favor with modern stick carpenters who use Speed Squares, mainly as

cutting aids with circular saws. Because they are making only square cuts on lumber, they don't need the versatility of the combination square. The sliding blade on the "combo" square is used for checking the depth and squareness of the sides of a mortise (impossible to do without a sliding blade or a second square), checking that a tenon cheek is parallel to a reference surface, and drawing a parallel line a set distance in from a reference edge. The square can also be placed on the surface of a timber to help keep a drill bit perpendicular to the timber's face.

Good combination squares are somewhat delicate and if dropped too many times can go out of whack, another reason they are seen more in shops than on job sites. If you have an old one from your grandpa, it can be adjusted back to square (if need be) by removing the blade from the stock and filing down one of the raised ridges the blade rides on. An auger bit file will fit the blade slot.

Specialty layout tools: There is a specialty tool specifically designed for edge reference in square rule layout: the Borneman layout template, named after Al Borneman, a machinist and timber-framing student. This tool has a fence (see facing page) that rides along the edge of the timber and has slots in ½-inch increments for drawing parallel lines a set distance from that edge. The tool is currently available through the Timber Framers Guild (see Resources), but if you are building only a frame or two, you could make your own from good-quality plywood, or just use your framing and combination squares.

Note that this tool assumes you have two adjacent and square reference faces on straight timbers; if you don't, you'll need to snap chalk lines and reference your squares (or the Borneman template) to those lines. To lay out mortises and tenons from a chalk line, you can file notches in a framing square, centered in the ends of

BORNEMAN LAYOUT TEMPLATE

the blade (for 2-inch mortises) and tongue (for 1½-inch) and at the opposite points on the heel (at the 1-inch and ¾-inch marks, respectively). These notches can then be used to register on the chalk line if it represents the centerline of the joint, or you can lay the edge of the framing square on the line if it represents the edges of the joint.

Templates can also be made out of plywood or hardboard for laying out angled cuts on braces and rafters, as long as you remember to hold the template against your reference plane. Often it is just as easy to use your framing square, as you'll see when we start laying out the timbers.

TIMBER TIP

Buy the best tool you can afford, but don't buy a tool until you need it.

THE FENCE ON THE BORNEMAN LAYOUT TEMPLATE *is ½ inch thicker on one side so you can either lay out whole number increments (2, 3, or 4 inches, etc.) or flip it over to shift the slots to half-inch increments.*

MARKING

Chalk line: This is used a lot in general carpentry but is mainly useful in timber framing for marking reference planes on curved or round timber. You can replace the thick twisted line in most new chalk boxes with braided backing (fly-fishing line) to get a finer chalk line. Red, yellow, and other chalk colors are permanent, so use only blue or white on timbers.

Carpenter's pencils: The thick lead on these pencils allows you to mark on rough timber without the point breaking. It should be sharpened to a flattened wedge shape so you can align the lead to make either a thin or thick line. The wide side of the pencil can also be shaved down flush to the lead on one side; this lets you get the lead in tight to your layout tool.

White chalk: Traditional "carpenter's chalk" comes in cake form but is hard to find these days; any schoolroom chalk will do. This can be used for indicating the reference faces of a timber and the arris (the edge shared by the two adjacent reference surfaces), as well as the number that locates the timber in the frame. You can also label the faces "top," "bottom," "east," "north," etc., to

CHALK LINE

CARPENTER'S CHALK

CARPENTER'S PENCILS & ERASER

TIMBER TIP

Use a solid line only to mark lines that are meant to be cut; use light tick marks to indicate other measurements. You may have to erase your marks later if they're on a visible surface, and a solid line is much more difficult to erase. Worse, you may cut the wrong line if there are too many on the timber. Don't use ink, felt markers, or crayons on your timber except on end grain or pieces to be cut off.

SHAPE A CARPENTER'S PENCIL *into a flattened wedge at the tip using your chisel, block plane, or knife.*

keep you oriented while the timber is on the sawhorses. Chalk washes off fairly easily, which is generally an advantage. You'll permanently label your timbers with a chisel or marker (on the end grain) at the end of cutting.

Erasers: White plastic erasers (like the Mars brand) seem to work best to remove pencil from wood if you make that rare mistake. A hand plane, scraper, or spokeshave will work if you are going to plane the surface anyway, but you will need to rough up the planed area to make it look the same as the rest of the timber, if it is staying rough: Lay a small handsaw blade flat across the planed area, and then bend it so the set on the teeth rough up the wood as you drag it back and forth a few strokes. A wire brush or a riffler-type rasp can also work.

OTHER TOOLS FOR LAYOUT

Timber handling is an important consideration in this work: you want to minimize the amount of heavy lifting and carrying you need to do, and make sure the timber is at a comfortable working height for layout and cutting.

Timber cart: If you're very good at planning your sequence of work and lucky enough to have a big work area, you may be able to stack your timbers in the order you need them so that you can lift them off and right over to your work station next to the pile. In reality, though, you'll probably be laying out a bunch of timbers before cutting to minimize the number of tools lying around underfoot, and your timber storage, layout, and cutting areas may be some distances apart. A cart makes it possible for just one person to move the largest timbers in the small frames included in this book. Carts can be homemade: a set of wheels and an axle can be adapted to a wooden frame, usually counterweighted or otherwise designed to keep it from flipping over when not carrying a timber.

Rollers: These can be used to help get timbers out of the stack, load them onto a truck or trailer, and move them around the building site.

THE TIMBER CART AND ROLLERS *shown here make moving timbers relatively easy for one person; this cart is rated for 500 pounds. It's also helpful to understand and use the principles of gravity, levers, and fulcrums to avoid having to lift the whole timber all at once.*

BUILDING A SAWHORSE

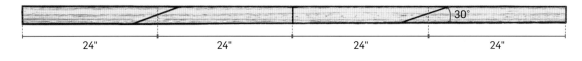

24" 24" 24" 24"

Legs from an 8-foot 2×4, with 30° cut for angled feet

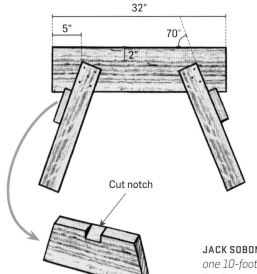

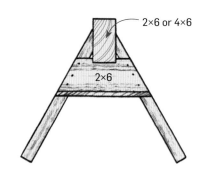

Cut notch

JACK SOBON'S LIGHT SAWHORSE DESIGN *calls for two 8-foot 2×4s and one 10-foot 2×6 to make one pair. A stouter 4×6 may be substituted for the top rail. Angled feet dig into soft ground. Horse height, here about 2 feet, is a matter of personal preference, but don't forget that you will be working on timbers 6 to 10 inches deep.*

Sawhorses: For timber framing, sawhorses should be shorter (24 to 28 inches off the ground) than conventional horses because of the deeper sections of timber, and because you may be climbing onto the timber for mortising, depending on the tool you use. This all depends on your own height, of course. Make sure the horses are heavy-duty and wide enough to allow you to roll over an 8×10 timber a few times. If you will be working on rough ground, like driveway gravel or grass, your horses should have splayed legs with square ends so the corners will dig into the ground. If you're on a wood deck or level concrete, cut the bottoms of the legs level (parallel to the ground) so they have more bearing and grip.

Cutting Tools

Here's where you'll have to make some decisions about what you can afford, how long you want to spend on construction, and how many frames you are going to build. Power tools can speed up the cutting process but are not necessarily more accurate or safer. They are certainly noisier, usually more expensive, and require a power source. Traditional timber framers can get by with an axe, a saw, a chisel, a mallet, and a hand drill or mortising chisel. Let's look at some reasonable options for the modern worker:

Saws: Cutting off the ends of large timbers requires a different saw than that used for joinery. A Western-style crosscut handsaw (8-point or coarser) can be used for large cuts. There are also large, aggressive Japanese handsaws that will do the job. End cuts are one place where a power saw might be preferable. A well-tuned chainsaw in the hands of a good operator can make very accurate cuts, at least good enough for ends that will be hidden (such as the end of a tenon or sill). Portable circular saws come in larger blade diameters, such as 10, 14, 16 and even 24 inches. Smaller circular saws, such as 7¼-inch (the most common) or 8-inch are versatile enough to be used for shoulder work and for roughing out tenons and housings. Set the depth slightly less than required and make multiple cross-grain kerfs (slots left by the saw blade), allowing the waste to be easily removed. There are also chainsaw attachments you can put on worm-drive circular saws. If you already have a 7¼-inch saw, I recommend adding a 10-inch to your tool kit; if you are buying just one saw, get an 8-inch.

For joinery in which the cuts need to be shallower and more accurate, I prefer a Japanese-style saw with finer teeth

CIRCULAR SAWS

(18-point or finer). These saws cut on the pull stroke, allowing the blade to be thinner.

Handsaws come with either *rip* or *crosscut* tooth patterns: ripsaw teeth are sharpened straight across and are used for cutting with the grain, while crosscut teeth are sharpened at alternating bevels and are best for cutting across the grain (cutting procedures are covered in chapter 5). You'll want both types of saws, although it's hard to find a Western-style rip saw in the hardware stores anymore. You can have a crosscut saw retoothed to a rip pattern, or get a Japanese saw; the Ryoba style has a rip blade on one side and crosscut on the other.

RIPSAW

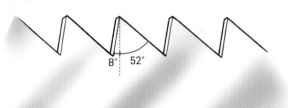

A ripsaw tooth is sharpened straight across. It has an angle of 60°: 8° from a perpendicular line dropped from the point of the tooth to the front, and 52° from the back of the tooth to the perpendicular.

CROSSCUT SAW

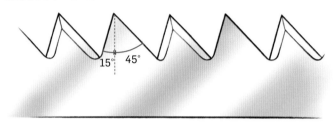

A crosscut saw tooth is sharpened at alternating bevels. It also has a total angle of 60°. However, the front angle is 15° and the back angle is 45°.

WESTERN-STYLE CROSSCUT TIMBER SAW
26 inches long with 3 teeth per inch (TPI)

JAPANESE CROSSCUT TIMBER SAW

RYOBA-STYLE JAPANESE SAW

Chisels: All of the mortises and tenons in our frames are 1½ inches thick, so that is the width of chisel you'll need. Timber-framing chisels are long and sturdy; the blade should be at least 7 inches long to get into deep mortises. Although the joinery can be roughed out with saws and drills, the chisel is used to pare the joint to the finished dimension. This one chisel is the workhorse of your tool kit.

Chisels can be purchased new or from antique tool dealers (see Resources). *Socket* chisels are more durable in this work than *tang* chisels. There are other types of chisels, such as *slicks* and *corner* chisels, that are somewhat useful but more difficult to sharpen. You can do all your work with the 1½-inch chisel and not have to carry around the extra tools. A hand plane can be used instead of a slick to flatten large areas, such as the cheeks of tenons. Sharpening is an important skill to learn; sharp tools make your work cleaner, quicker, easier, safer, and more accurate. See page 179 for sharpening tips.

Mallets: A 2- to 3-pound mallet is used to strike the chisel when removing lots of material and when driving pins. I recommend a flat-faced mallet made of wood (make your own) or one with an iron head faced with rawhide. Some framers prefer a cylindrical shape (like a carver's mallet), but I find that it rolls off the chisel when striking, and this could lead to wrist problems down the road. Don't use a dead-blow mallet (with shot sliding around in the head); you want to feel the chisel's cutting action in your hand, and a dead-blow mallet changes the feel of the chisel by absorbing some of the impact force. A commander (also called a *beetle* or *persuader*) is a large, 10- to 20-pound mallet used to drive timbers together during assembly. This can be home-made, using the end of a timber and fashioning a long handle from a tree branch, or you can purchase a dead-blow mallet in this case.

TIMBER TIP

If you have a woodworking shop already, you might be tempted to figure out ways of cutting timbers using your existing table saws, bandsaws, and "chop" saws. But remember that you want to minimize timber handling, and for big wood it's generally better to bring the tool to the workpiece rather than the other way around.

HOMEMADE 3-POUND WOODEN MALLET

1½-INCH SOCKET TIMBER FRAMING CHISEL

3-POUND IRON MALLET *with rawhide faces*

Planes: There are myriad styles of planes out there, but the most useful for timber framers is the *block* plane, used to chamfer edges of timbers and tenons and even to sharpen your pencil. A *bench rabbet* plane (such as the Stanley #10 series) can be used to clean up the corner between a tenon cheek and the shoulder. A *scrub* or *smoothing* plane has a curved blade and is useful if you want to hand plane the faces of your rough timbers (more on planing later).

You can buy your timbers planed, or ship them to a mill that does it, but this is expensive, and you'll probably have to clean them up anyway before the raising. Leaving the timbers rough-sawn is okay for barns and outbuildings, and you may not object to it in your house, but be aware that rough timbers seem to attract dust and cobwebs and won't accept a finish well. Hand planing can be a pleasurable experience and produces a slightly scalloped surface, but it takes a while and requires some elbow grease. Portable power planers make the job go more quickly, but they can leave machine marks unless you go slowly and carefully. These planers come in versions 4, 6, and 12 inches wide; the narrower ones require some tricky handling to avoid ridges when planing wider surfaces but might be useful for other carpentry jobs. Most pro timber framers use a 12-inch-wide model, but these are probably too expensive for just one frame, unless you can find a used one or a rental. In general, most of the specialized power tools for timber framing have good resale value on Internet venues (see Resources).

Spokeshave: This is really a type of plane; it has a small blade and side handles and is used to smooth out curved surfaces, such as on our joist and rafter reductions. It can also be used to smooth curved braces.

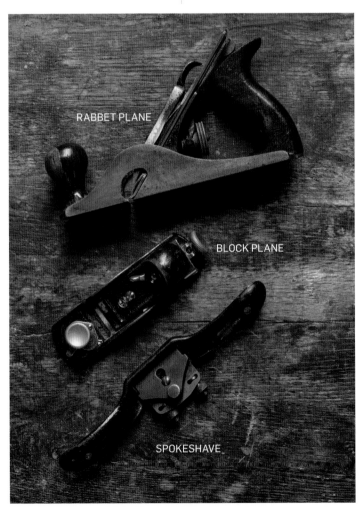

RABBET PLANE

BLOCK PLANE

SPOKESHAVE

ADZE

FELLING AXE

2-LB AXE

BROADAXE

Boring Tools

Mortising has always been a bigger challenge than making tenons, which can be cut with an axe or saw. Before drills, there were mortising chisels (still available) that had thick, narrow blades for starting a mortise from scratch and digging down to the depth required. Some traditional methods used axes exclusively and involved half-lap joinery for their connections, no mortise and tenon at all.

Our frames use 1½-inch mortises of various depths; some go completely through the timber (called *through mortises*). These are usually bored out with 1½-inch drill bits, then squared up with a chisel. You could drill multiple holes with smaller bits, but this is a lot of extra work in a project that is already labor-intensive. The most common method to bore is with an electric drill with a ½-inch chuck, auger bit, and extension. There is a lot of torque involved, so use a heavy-duty, low-RPM drill, like a Milwaukee Hole Hawg, and make sure the drill is designed to take the diameter of bit you're using.

Traditional alternatives include T-augers and boring machines (also called beam drills). These are still available

Axe: A small axe (about 20 inches long with a 2-pound head) can be used for roughing out joinery quickly, just like kerfing with a saw. If you aren't using power tools, an axe is a good addition to your toolbox. *Broadaxes* are used to finish hand-hewn timbers that have been roughly squared (juggled) with a *felling* axe.

Adze: This tool has a long handle and a curved head with a 3- to 5-inch-wide cutting edge. It is swung between the legs to shape timbers or boards while standing over them. In our frame we use the adze to reduce the depth of joists and rafters at their end joints while creating a pleasing curve that was previously roughed out with an axe and will be finished afterward with a spokeshave.

(with the 1½-inch bits required) through antique tool dealers and don't require power.

Electric drills have some significant drawbacks: they won't run perpendicular to the surface without constant attention, and if the hole is not cleaned out frequently, the bit can jam up with chips and send you for a loop. An auger bit is designed to carry the chips up and out of the holes, but sometimes, especially with green wood, the chips get stuck above the cutting head. Then the bit can't turn so the drill body does instead, taking the operator with it. This can be quite a surprise and hard on the wrists and arms if you aren't prepared for it. Some framers use Forstner-type bits with self-feeding screws at the tip; these are readily available in the diameters required but are even more likely to clog up without

repeatedly withdrawing the bit to clean out the hole. The ideal bit is a long auger bit with 6 to 7 inches of twist, but these can be hard to find. You may be tempted to cut off an antique T-auger bit and chuck it up in an electric drill, but they were not designed for that and could break.

The power tool of choice for most timber framers (and usually the first one they buy) is a chain mortiser, which has a 1½-inch bar and chain that plunges in to create the mortise. It has a base that registers it perpendicular to the face it sits on.

CHAIN MORTISER

ELECTRIC DRILL

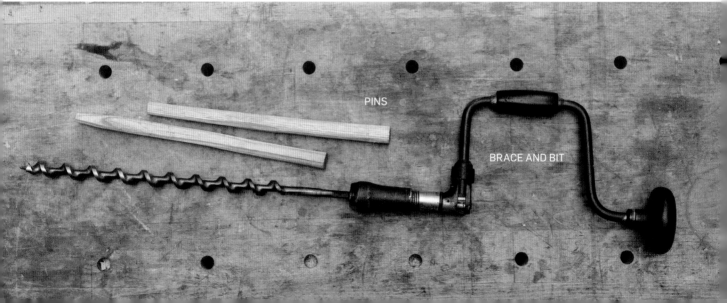

PINS

BRACE AND BIT

BORING MACHINE

A HOMEMADE TENON CHECKER *can be useful to make sure tenons aren't too thick, a common problem for beginners. You may have pared down to your layout lines on the edges but not in the middle of the tenon cheek.*

For drilling the pin holes, you'll want a longer (12 to 18 inches or so) auger bit in both ¾- and 1-inch diameters. Pin holes get drilled all the way through from one reference face so the pin stays straight, but through mortises are drilled halfway through from opposite sides. You can use a hand brace or electric drill to drill the pin holes, but the hand brace can't generate enough torque for use on larger-diameter mortises.

If you're just going to cut one frame, then a good ½-inch (that's the chuck size) drill with a side handle is probably the most economical (under $150),

and can also be used for drilling pin holes. Irwin and Greenlee make 1½-inch-diameter auger bits. A good antique boring machine can be had for $200 to $700 from one of the antique tool dealers mentioned in the Resources section. These are much preferable to electric drills because of their excellent resale value, safety, and ease of use. If you are cutting more than one frame, a chain mortiser is a worthwhile investment and can also be resold easily, but it will run from $1,600 to $3,400 (new), depending on the brand. Refurbished or used tools may be available through tool dealers

or by searching or placing an ad in the Timber Framers Guild newsletter (see Resources).

Tenon checker: Most timber-framing novices start out making their mortises too tight and their tenons too thick, perhaps for fear of taking too much material away. Mortises can be checked for width with the 1½-inch tongue of the framing square. For tenons, take a piece of plywood or thick, rigid Plexiglas and jigsaw very accurately a 1½-inch slot about 10 inches long. You can use this to slip over the tenon to check its final thickness.

CHAPTER 5

PROCEDURES FOR LAYOUT & CUTTING

It's a beautiful day to start your timber frame. Your timbers have been delivered and they're neatly stacked and stickered. Your sturdy and faithful sawhorses stand ready. Set them as level to each other as possible; not only will you be more comfortable, but since you'll tend to saw and drill plumb, even on sloped ground, this will help your accuracy.

First Steps in Layout

1 **Begin by labeling the frame plan** from one side of the building to the other. You will use your labeled frame as a guide when you label each timber. We'll use *numbers* to mark the bents (the cross frames of timbers perpendicular to the roof ridge), *Roman numerals* for the bays (the spaces between bents), and *letters* to indicate the walls (the lines of posts running 90 degrees to the bents).

This code will help you visualize each timber in the frame as you work and will also help identify it on raising day as you are hunting through the pile for the next piece to go up. Some pieces (braces, joists, rafters) are identical and interchangeable, but others will have subtle differences, such as fewer mortises, or faces with defects you're trying to hide. The label on a timber indicates its location and orientation within the frame. (So, for example, a post in the second bent on wall B would be labeled "2B.") Girts, plates, and ties are labeled according to their bent or bay, and their ends marked with the code of the piece they are going into (unless they are interchangeable).

It doesn't matter what system you use as long as you're consistent and can avoid duplication. You'll label the timber with white chalk once you get it on the horses, then permanently mark it on the end grain with a felt marker or crayon after it is cut. Traditionally, carpenters marked the faces of timbers with a chisel or gouge and used a Roman numeral system with "flags" or other symbols attached to the numbers to further distinguish locations.

LABELING THE FRAME

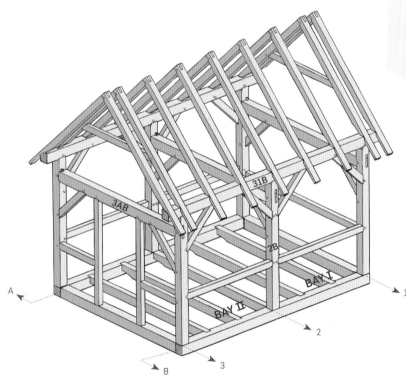

THE LABELING SYSTEM YOU DEVELOP FOR YOUR FRAME *will keep you oriented while you're working on individual timbers and will make the raising more efficient.*

2 Decide which timber in the frame you are going to work on, and **determine shoulder-to-shoulder length from drawings**. Add tenon lengths (if any) to find overall length needed. This step can be done before you go out to the timber stack. Remember that the shoulder-to-shoulder length is what is critical, not overall length. If a tenon is a little short, no big deal; if it's a little long, it can be trimmed. Shoulder-to-shoulder lengths for most pieces are provided in chapter 6.

TIMBER TIP

Shoulder-to-shoulder length is the critical dimension. Calculate and use it to lay out the timber, leaving enough length to add tenons later.

FRENCH CARPENTER'S MARKS

ALPHABET DU CHARPENTIER.

ON MANY HISTORIC TIMBER FRAMES *around the world, you'll find carpenters' marks made in chalk or incised into the timbers with chisels, gouges, or knives. Various systems were used; the French have used Roman numerals and other symbols to indicate orientation of timbers, location in the frame, waste to be cut, centerlines, and more. This system is still in use today.*

3 Take the appropriate piece from your timber inventory. Keep in mind its eventual location in the frame. You may want to get all similar timbers out at the same time — for example, work on all the sills at the same time, then joists, then posts, etc.

4 With the timber on horses, **look down the length of the timber to identify crowned surfaces (if any)**. On horizontal members, such as sills, crown should usually face up to resist vertical loading; vertical members in a plane should have any crowns facing the same direction, either in or out. Posts that have a severe crown (more than ¼ inch over their length), should not be used on an exterior, where the crowning could cause the sheathing to bulge. If you have crowned joists or rafters, you should group them together (crown up) in the center of the building so the floor or roof has a gradual "hump." If the crown is too severe, you'll have to snap a chalk line and then plane or saw to the line. Usually, this is only necessary on a reference face. You can then use the chalk line as reference to lay out the housings for the perfect timber on the opposite non-reference face.

5 Check for wind, or twist, of the timber. You can do this by **setting two straight-edges (framing squares work well) on the ends of the timber (where the end joinery will be) and sighting across the tops.** If the straightedges are out of parallel by more than ⅛ inch over 12 feet, you should fix that face and its adjacent reference face by planing (at least where the joinery occurs) or get another piece. If necessary, you can snap chalk lines to represent square reference planes to work off of, but this gets into advanced technique and takes experience; some timber framers work exclusively off of snap lines and don't trust the edges. Take the time to find a good sawyer, and you may not have any timbers that are so far out of square, twisted, or crowned that you need to use snap lines.

5

6 Check actual vs. nominal dimensions, and identify the two adjacent surfaces that will be the reference faces (they must be square to each other). **Make a V on each of these faces pointing to the arris,** the edge shared by both.

Reference faces are dimensional benchmarks. On horizontal members, the top surface is usually a reference face (floor level, roof surface, etc.). Outside faces are also usually reference faces. A corner post, for example, must have its two outside faces as the reference faces. For timbers where this top or outside face guideline is not applicable, choose some other way to keep track so that these reference faces are oriented the same way; we traditionally use the north and/or west faces.

Keep appearance in mind when selecting reference faces: they are often hidden, so the best-looking faces are often not reference faces. Faces with staining can be oriented so that they are hidden or covered. Timbers with large knots in the middle of the length are not as structurally sound as clearer pieces, so they could be used over a partition wall (framed with studs to help carry the

6

load) or where the load is less, such as a gable end rafter. Timbers will usually check toward the face that's closest to the pith. This is cosmetic and doesn't affect the strength. If you find it objectionable, you can orient that face so that it's hidden. This may seem like a lot to consider, but the point is that *nothing is random.* Without being obsessive (or developing "analysis paralysis"), you want to evaluate the timber for its best orientation.

Using reference faces (instead of centerlines) from which to measure joinery assures that all timbers on the outside of the building will have flush surfaces for the application of sheathing. This exercise also helps you visualize your "castle

The arris where the two reference surfaces meet is marked with a chalked V.

in the air" — it's critical that you always know what your timber will look like in the finished frame in order to avoid mistakes. Once the reference faces are identified, you should be able to visualize which end of the timber is which.

7

7 Lay your measuring tape along the arris and locate principle joinery as well as the ends of the timber when cut to length.
Adjust the tape back and forth (assuming you have extra length) to avoid knots and other defects. Mark initial joinery positions as determined from drawings, using light, short marks to indicate the control point each joint will have. This point will usually be a centerline or side of the joint, depending on how it is dimensioned in the drawings. Don't draw heavy lines where unnecessary, as you may have to clean them off later. And remember: only draw solid lines that are meant to be cut. Once you're happy with the location of all the joinery, put the tape measure away and pick up your rigid layout tool (framing square, combination square, or Borneman layout template) to lay out individual joints, always registering the tool to reference faces.

Laying Out the Mortise and Tenon

As an example, let's lay out the mortise-and-tenon joint that joins the sills that we looked at in chapter 3. The procedures explained here will apply to other joints in the frame as well.

THE MORTISE

As explained in the section on square rule (page 35), the mortise in the long sill will have a housing to accept the reduced width of the short sill. This housing will be laid out 7½ inches from the outside reference face.

1 First, holding a framing square on the arris mark representing the end of the long sill timber, **square lines around all four faces to indicate the eventual end cut.** Hold the framing square along the arris by grasping it in the middle so you are getting a line truly square to the edge. If there is a knot or chip of wood causing the square to rock, instead of holding the inside edge of the square against the arris, bring it onto the top surface of the timber and align the outside edge of the square to the arris.

JOINERY DETAIL

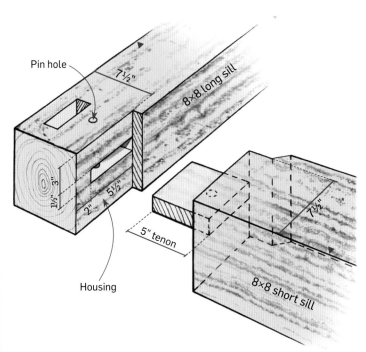

Pin hole

7½"

8×8 long sill

3"

1½"

5½"

2"

Housing

5" tenon

7½"

8×8 short sill

1

2 Without moving the square, **make a mark 7½ inches in from the end line,** then slide the square down and carry that mark to the inside face; this is the inside edge of the housing where the short sill enters. Square this line down the inside face from the top reference face.

2

3 Next, pick up your combination square and set the blade to 7½ inches (or use the Borneman template) and **mark the back of the housing** on the top face.

3

4 Using the same tool, **draw lines down 3 inches and 4½ inches from the top** on the inside face to represent the mortise.

5 Note how the mortise (and corresponding tenon on the short sill) is 2 inches short of the end of the timber so that it is not open where moisture could get in. We call this leaving the relish. To draw the relish, hold the 5½-inch mark on the framing square on the inside of the housing line, or **use the 2-inch body of the square registered to the end-cut line.**

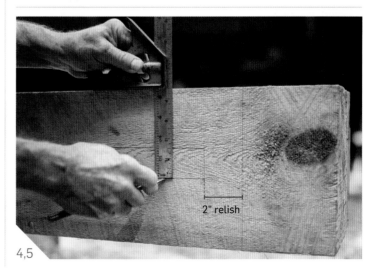

2" relish

4,5

6 Roll the timber over to **complete the same layout on the adjacent side,** always making sure you are measuring and drawing lines from either the top or outside reference face.

7 Finally, lay out the pin hole on the top reference face; pins are (almost) always drilled from the reference face in square rule because the mortise is closer to that side. The joints for the sill corners and center joist get 1-inch-diameter pins since these are long (5-inch) tenons. These pin holes get laid out 1½ inches off of the shoulder line and centered on the mortise. **Use the 1½-inch width of the tongue on the framing square for this layout, with 2¾ inches held on the inside of the housing** (half of a 5½-inch wide mortise).

TIMBER TIP

Nothing is random. Any decision you make about the layout of the timber — which face is exposed, where the joinery occurs, how the piece is oriented — should have a reason behind it. If you find yourself saying, "It doesn't matter," think again. Be careful not to take it too far, however, and end up in "analysis paralysis."

2¾"

7

When to Plane

Planing your timbers for appearance after the joinery is cut could affect the final dimensions of the frame. Instead, you should plane visible reference faces *before* you do layout, remembering to keep adjacent faces square to each other as you plane. Reference faces that are going to be covered by sheathing or flooring don't need to be planed, since they will be hidden. Non-reference faces can be planed *after* cutting without affecting dimensions, since the housings establishing the perfect-timber-within are well below the surface. The main purpose of the planing here is to get rid of saw and pencil marks and blemishes from shoe prints and the like and to create a smooth surface. Some people prefer the rough-sawn look and don't plane at all, but these surfaces tend to pick up dust and cobwebs more readily. All timbers shown in this book are rough sawn.

THE TENON

The tenon layout on the short sill mirrors the mortise layout. If the end of the timber is fairly square, you may not need an end cut since the end of the tenon is buried in the mortise and not a critical length.

1 **Determine the shoulder-to-shoulder length** of the short sills (10 feet 9 inches) to locate the tenons on each end, keeping in mind other joinery in the sill and avoiding knots and other defects where possible.

2 **Add 4⅞ inches to each end** to account for the length of the tenons, and square this line around the timber. This is the timber cutoff line.

3 Square the shoulder line down 3 inches from the top of the timber, **leaving a 1½-inch space below to indicate tenon thickness.** Continue the line down to the bottom of the timber to mark the lower shoulder.

4 Use your combination square (or Borneman template) to **draw parallel lines at 3 inches and 4½ inches to represent the tenon "cheeks."**

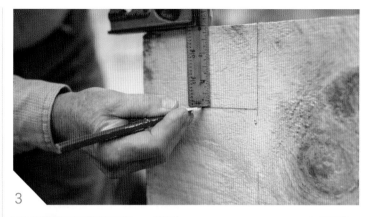

3

4

Keep in mind throughout the cutting process that some of your layout lines may disappear with the cutoff, so reestablish those lines if necessary on the new surface after each cut. There's no need to lay out the reduction and the 2-inch relish to be cut off the tenon, nor the pin hole on the tenon, until the tenon cheeks are made.

It's a good idea to work with another person, not just to help move timbers, but also to have him or her check your layout before cutting. Remember that parts of the joinery — tables (faces) of housings, cheeks and faces of tenons, sides of mortises — are usually parallel to the reference faces (exceptions might be parts of rafter and brace joints that come in at an angle). Keep this in mind when you're transferring lines around the timber onto non-reference faces that are out of square, or when setting up boring tools to drill holes from these faces.

Cutting Procedures

We'll go deeper into the specifics of laying out each joint when we get to the frame details in chapter 6, but for now let's discuss the general procedures for cutting. Joinery design (as we'll see later) derives from an understanding of the anisotropic nature of wood. So, too, do techniques for cutting the joinery: the wood's directional grain determines how it can be most efficiently cut and shaped and how it will resist the stresses imposed on it.

In the layout phase, you located your joinery to avoid most knots and other defects; this will make cutting much easier as you work the clear and predictable grain. The proper sequence of saw, drill, and chisel work generally involves severing the long wood fibers to a certain depth (crosscutting or boring), which then allows you to easily split out (rip) parallel to the grain, thus removing a large hunk of wood to that depth. This technique is similar for both mortises and tenons.

Hold That Saw!

TIPS TO REMEMBER BEFORE YOU CUT

→ Locate all joinery before cutting either end so that you can move joints if need be. (You can make a shallow saw kerf at one end before layout to help secure the tape measure at your starting point.)

→ As a rule of thumb, cut the most difficult joinery first. If you make a mistake or aren't happy with the results, you may have a chance to re-mark the piece or get another before you have spent a lot of time on it.

→ Wait to make the second end cut. By leaving one end long for a while, you may also be leaving yourself a way to save the timber if you make an error.

→ If the end of the timber has a tenon, the end-of-tenon cut does not have to be perfect. All tenon lengths are cut $1/8$ inch under nominal to be sure they don't bottom out in the mortise.

→ Work your way down the timber, cutting joinery as you go and trying to do as much as you can on one face before rolling the timber. Economy of movement becomes very important to a timber framer; perform all similar operations on a given timber face at one time.

→ When cutting the end of a timber, if a large or long piece of waste is going to be released, make sure that it's supported or that someone is ready to catch it to avoid torn grain as the piece pulls away under its own weight. When catching a waste piece, keep your feet out from under the fall line and direct the weight down and away from the sawyer as the cut is completed to keep the kerf from binding the saw blade.

→ Always be aware which sides of the timber will be visible in the finished frame so you can be extra careful when working the exposed faces.

CUTTING THE MORTISE

When cutting mortises, "sawr it, score it, and bore it." Saw any housing shoulders first, then score the sides of the mortise before boring it out. This will prevent tearout from the bit traveling onto a visible surface. Bore the end holes of the mortise before boring out the wood in between and chiseling out the waste. If the mortise is near the end of the timber, finish the mortise before cutting off the end so that as you work the mortise you avoid blowing out the end grain.

1 **Cut the housing shoulder.** This first step is important because it establishes a clean, accurate juncture between the mating pieces. You can then use the boring machine and other tools without worrying about straying past the joint line, since it is easy to see and the fibers have already been cut. Using a fine-toothed saw, carefully cut down to the exact depth of the housing; you may even want to score the pencil line first with a knife to get an even cleaner cut.

THE FINISHED SILL MORTISE AND HOUSING (above) is started by cutting the housing shoulder (below).

1

TIMBER TIP

Cut or score a shoulder line before boring a mortise so that the boring bit doesn't tear grain out over the layout line. Finish a mortise completely before removing the housing so you have a good surface to reference from for depth.

2 **Score the mortise sides.** Work your way around the edges of the mortise, outlining it with your chisel and mallet. This will help guide the bit.

3 **Bore the mortise.** Set up the boring machine or chain mortiser, making sure you're boring square to your reference faces. Sometimes this requires shimming the machine if you're on a non-reference face. If you're using an electric drill, you may want to have a helper hold a framing square on the face so you can align your drill bit parallel to it; you'll use this same technique when boring pin holes. Here it becomes important to have your timber level on the horses, which complements your natural tendency to drill plumb. If the timber is very level, you could actually mount a bubble level on your drill to guide you plumb (some drills have built-in bubble levels for the same purpose).

Bore the end holes of the mortise first (3b), setting the depth by marking the drill bit with tape (if using a portable drill). If you're using a boring machine or chain mortiser, you need to lower the bit to the surface to set the depth stop, making sure to add the length of

2

3a

the feed screw or curve of the chain bar to get full diameter at the proper depth. You will need to add the housing depth to the nominal depth of the mortise to determine the actual depth to set your boring tool to. Keep in mind that the housings are not necessarily ½ inch deep; they will differ depending on how oversized or undersized your timber is. For example, if this sill timber is 8¼ inches wide instead of a nominal 8 inches, the housing will be framed

3b

4a

4b

7½ inches from the outside reference face, so the housing will be ¾ inch deep as measured from the inside (non-reference) face. Thus the mortise will be bored 5¾ inches deep (slightly more is okay, but no less).

Bore holes in between the end holes, but don't overlap holes, as this could cause the bit to wander. You can overlap holes if you are using a chain mortiser, though. Because of the curve of the chain, you may want to add ½ to ¾ inch to the depth so you don't need to clean up the bottom.

4 Square up the mortise. If not using a chain mortiser, you'll need to square up the sides of the holes you've just bored since a drill bit is round and your goal is a rectangular hole. Remove remaining wood with your chisel, always severing the grain by crosscutting before paring parallel to the grain. Using your mallet, **drive the chisel down the ends of the mortise** (with the bevel of the chisel toward the inside of the mortise)(4a). Then set the mallet down and, using hand power and a little upper body weight, **pare down the sides** (4b). Alternate between cutting the end grain and paring the sides until you've reached the bottom.

As you cut, be careful to keep the bearing surfaces of the mortise and housing square to the surface; in the case of the mortise on the long sill, the bearing surface is the bottom where the tenon of the short sill rests. Other sides of the mortise can taper away a bit (no more than ⅛ inch).

5 **Check squareness (and the depth)** with your combination square, and use the appropriate leg of a framing square to check the width. Make sure the sides of the mortise are parallel to the reference face; you can use your framing and combination squares in "combination" to check this.

The mortise is cut first and finished before the housing because you need a good surface to bear on when checking its depth and squareness and to rest your boring tool on. If the mortise is at the end of the timber, as in our corner sill joint, finish the mortise completely before cutting off the end of the timber and creating the housing. This will allow you to work the mortise with less chance of blowing out the relish.

6 Cut off the end of the timber and **draw the housing line around the end grain.**

7 **Kerf and chisel the housing to its finished depth (7a–c).** The interior of the table, or face, of the housing can be hollowed out a bit (⅛ inch or so) so the shoulder of the tenoned piece meets the housing line tightly (7d). This is also done because, when green boxed heart timber shrinks tangentially, the outside shrinks the most, and the housing face will want to bulge up slightly.

6

5

7a

7b

7c

7d

8 Drill the pin holes. The pin holes on the mortises get drilled directly on the mark and straight through all the way; the tenons will get the offset for drawboring. Be careful not to blow out the other side of the timber as you bore through. You or a friend can keep an eye out for the feed screw of the bit breaking through; often you can feel or hear it. To keep your bit aligned square to the reference face, use a combination square or some other guide. A mirror also works well, as you can see any dogleg and just need to tip the bit back and forth until the reflection is aligned.

TIMBER TIP

Pin holes get drilled all the way through from the reference face; through mortises get drilled halfway from opposite faces.

8

How to Cut Accurately with a Handsaw

Novices can often make a better cut with a handsaw than a portable circular saw; because the former is slower, you have more time to correct any error as you go. Start at the arris on the far side of the timber, and place the saw just to the waste side of the pencil line. Saw teeth are bent slightly, or *set*, outward from the body, alternating left and right, so that the kerf the saw makes is wider than the body of the saw, thus allowing the saw to drop through the cut. You want the teeth that are angled toward the pencil line to remove about half of it, so most of the saw should be outside the line.

Draw backward lightly on the saw to get it started at the corner (the arris), using your thumb as a fence to keep the saw from jumping around (A). By starting at the corner, you remove only a small amount of wood, and the cutting is easy as you get the kerf started. Don't try to cut across the whole face of the piece at the beginning.

As you cut, lower the handle of the saw to cut at an angle across the top face without going down the far side, which you can't see (B). When you reach the upper corner nearer you, keep to the line you have just made across the top as you saw down the vertical line facing you. Once you reach the bottom of the timber in the front, you will have made half the desired cut. To continue cutting down the back vertical line, stop and go around to the other side of the timber in order to watch that line as you cut it (C). The kerf you made on the first side will help guide your saw.

Simply by seeing what you are doing and paying attention, you can cut very accurately instead of hoping that the saw is cutting true on the blind side. Of course, all this advice assumes that your saw is correctly sharpened and set.

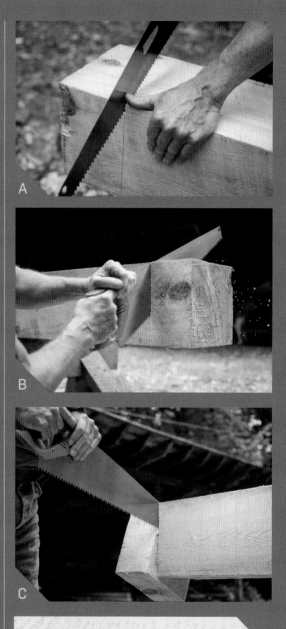

A

B

C

TIMBER TIP

Don't cut a line you can't see.

CUTTING THE TENON

Work one side of the tenon at a time. You'll start shaping the tenon by first crosscutting the shoulder line down to the cheek using a saw. This is a critical cut, so take your time (perfect is good enough).

1

1 **Make the shoulder cut with a circular saw or crosscut saw.** You might be tempted to stay away from the shoulder line $1/16$ inch or so to be safe and then pare down to it with your chisel, but paring end grain is difficult, and if you have hundreds of shoulders to cut, you'll soon learn to make your first cut accurate.

2 Once the shoulder cuts have been made, **split out the waste block to the tenon line.** Do the cheek of the tenon closest to the reference face first, using one of three techniques:

• Use your chisel to split out sections.

• Use an axe, handsaw, or portable circular saw to kerf and then use your chisel and mallet to knock out the blocks between kerfs.

• Use a ripsaw; this is the best option when there are knots or wild grain.

Kerfing with a Circular Saw

Set the depth of the circular saw to $1/16$ inch above the layout line and make multiple kerfs about $1/2$ inch apart. If you're on a non-reference face, be sure to set the saw to the shallowest depth, since the depth will vary across the timber if the face is not square.

A

B

I prefer the first method if the wood is clear and straight-grained (planned for during layout): **Place the chisel bevel-side-down at an angle across a corner on the end grain of the waste to be removed.** Since you've severed the grain at the shoulder, driving in the chisel with a mallet should remove a chunk of wood all the way to the shoulder cut (2a).

2a

Now look at the way the grain slopes. If it rises toward the shoulder, you can be pretty confident that you can continue to remove material without splitting down into the tenon. If the grain goes down, you'll have to be more careful and switch directions, or go cross-grain, or start paring as you get close to the tenon cheek. As you remove large pieces, **go halfway down to the cheek line each time;** when you get to within ⅛ inch of the line, you can start paring.

2b

Orient your chisel according to what you want to accomplish with it: To remove a large amount of material, go bevel-down and strike the chisel with your mallet (2b). Placing the bevel down causes the chisel to rise up in the cut and keeps it from diving down into the material. But when it comes time to pare or finely trim the surface, flip the chisel over so its flat bottom acts as a guide.

TIMBER TIP

Both the tenon and the mortise should be shaped to be parallel with the grain of their respective members.

3 When you're within ⅛ inch of the tenon's side lines (those running parallel to the grain) **use a corner of the chisel to pare a bevel** (chamfer) on the edges of the tenon down to the cheek line, again leaving half the line. This chamfering removes just a bit of material at a time, giving you more control to get the perimeter of the tenon perfect. Then you can pare the main part of the tenon, staying away from the finished edges and using the chamfers as a guide for depth.

Be careful not to pare all the way across the tenon from just one side; you could tear out the other side and lose your cheek line. Always work from the edges in toward the center. When paring, keep both hands behind the cutting edge by gripping the

3

blade with the forward hand and using it to brace against the side of the timber as you steer and push with the rear hand on the end of the handle. For finer shavings, try making a slicing cut by pivoting the chisel in your forward hand as you push with the rear hand. For more aggressive action (but less control), move both hands to the end of the handle. Avoid letting your forward hand move out in front to hold the timber — if you're having to push so hard that the timber is moving, you probably need to sharpen your chisel.

More Tenon Paring

Besides using a chisel, you can also pare tenon cheeks with a hand plane (though it must be a rabbet plane to work right up to a tenon shoulder) or with a slick if it's a very large tenon or a scarf joint.

4 **Check your tenon's distance down from the reference face using your combination or framing square;** it should be 3 inches down from the top surface of the sill (and the same for floor joist tenons). All the rest of the tenon cheeks on this frame are 1½ inches from the reference face, except for the barefaced tenons on 4×5s (wall girts and door posts).

4

5 Roll the timber and finish the opposite side of the tenon, **checking it until the tenon tester just slips on all the way to the shoulder.**

5

6 Lay out and cut the reduction. Because the tenon of the short sill is going into a non-reference face of the long sill, it needs to be reduced to the 7½-inch perfect-timber-within. This reduction is cut on the inside (non-reference) face of the short sill. Use your combination square to **measure 7½ inches from the reference face and draw a line down the length of the tenon and up the shoulder** (6a).

Carry this reduction back far enough to clear the housing on the widest mating timber. Although these housings are nominally ½ inch deep, they

6a

could be as much as ¾ or 1 inch, depending on how much variation your sawyer has provided. To be safe, we usually make these reductions, on all tenoned members, 1½ inches back from the shoulder.

After coming out the 1½ inches, lay out a 45-degree bevel to the surface of the timber rather than making a square notch. You could also make this a gradual curve, using an adze and spokeshave. Carry these lines around to the opposite side of the tenon. **Use a rip saw to cut the reduction** (6b), and then **chisel out the remaining triangle of wood to create the 45-degree bevel** (6c).

Note that this reduction only occurs on tenoned pieces going into non-reference faces that have housings cut to meet the perfect-timber-within. Post bottoms, for example, don't get reduced because they are resting on reference faces (top of sill) that represent the perfect timber. An exception would be where girts or braces enter a reference face with a similar member coming from the opposite side. Then we might house the tenoned end into the reference face for aesthetics to make it match the other side. (See Rules of Thumb for Joinery Design in Square Rule, page 78.)

6b

6c

A Perfect Fit

How tight should a finished mortise and tenon joint be? Both the mortise and tenon will shrink somewhat, but it's hard to predict how much or if it will be the same amount. Too tight a fit can cause a joint to split during assembly, raising, or seasoning; too loose is, well, sloppy, and can result in stepped surfaces where timbers should be flush. However, plenty of clearance is helpful and sometimes essential during raising when many joints must come together at once. You should strive for a perfect, sliding fit, at least over the last inch or two as the joint is pulled together.

7 Measure and lay out the 2-inch relish on the other side of the tenon. **Cut it with a rip saw,** first making a crosscut kerf at the shoulder. This step is only required on tenons that enter mortises at the very end of the receiving timber. In our case only the sills meet this description, but if we didn't have a 1-foot roof overhang, we would also leave a relish where the posts enter the ends of the plates.

8 **Taper the tenon** (except for a bearing surface, which, in this case, is the bottom) starting about halfway out from the shoulder, reducing the thickness and width about ⅛ inch at the ends (8a). This makes the tenon slip more easily into the mortise.

Lightly chamfer the end to reduce the danger of a chip splitting off as it enters the mortise (8b).

TIMBER TIP

Cut tenons a bit (⅛ inch) shorter than nominal — or cut mortises that much deeper — to avoid having the tenon bottom out.

7

8a

8b

9 Lay out and drill the pin hole on the cheek of the tenon closest to the reference face. **Use the 1½-inch tongue of the square placed against the shoulder** (9a), making sure the shoulder is square to the reference face. Locate the center of the tenon and make a mark, then **offset this mark ⅛ inch (for drawbore) toward the shoulder to locate the drill tip** (9b).

9a

9b

THE PIN HOLE ON A TENON *is offset about ⅛ inch toward the shoulder to pull the joint tight as the pin is driven.*

TIMBER TIP

Clean up your cut timber by erasing any pencil marks on surfaces that will be visible, or by planing. Label the timber on the end grain and lightly chamfer its edges with a block plane before taking it to the "done" pile. This last step will help prevent splinters when carrying the timbers.

DRAWBORING

Some timber framers drawbore, offsetting the holes in the mortise and tenon slightly to cause the joint to draw up tight. Others avoid drawboring, as it requires a bit more work and thinking. It's well established by tradition, however, and it intrigues many people new to the craft. Drawboring causes the pin to bend slightly as it goes through the tenon, pulling the joint together snugly as it is driven through. As the timbers shrink, the pin then acts as a spring to keep the joint tight. Assemblies pulled together with come-alongs and then drilled without drawboring will never get any tighter, and the joints are free to open up as the mortised piece shrinks.

Pins for any kind of drawboring are heavily tapered on one end so the point can catch the far-side hole after diversion by the offset hole in the tenon. While some pin holes are blind for aesthetic or other reasons, most are bored right through to allow the tapered end of a pin to be driven far enough to yield full or nearly full diameter at the exit side.

Sometimes a drawbored pin hole should be offset in two directions, as with sloped members like braces and rafters. One way to think about it is to visualize which way you want the mortised timber to be drawn, and then offset the hole in the tenon in that direction. Measure for the pin layout using the framing square; traditionally, pin holes in square rule layout are centered 1½ or 2 inches from the shoulder of the joint.

The amount of offset for the drawbore in softwoods should be a heavy ⅛ inch for ¾-inch pins, and a light ⅛ inch for 1-inch pins, which can't bend as much. Tenons with lots of relish beyond the pin hole (more than 3 inches) can be drawbored more than shorter tenons. Hardwoods should be drawbored a bit less than softwoods. Most novices tend to overdo the offset, so test-fit a few joints at the start of your project to see how you're doing.

During assembly, be sure to look through each joint's pin hole to see if the holes are offset just slightly, and in the right direction. If less than two-thirds of the tenon's hole is visible, you'll need to elongate it a bit with a long ¼-inch chisel, or put a very long, sharp point on the pin. If less than half the hole is visible, or if you drawbored in the wrong direction, it's best to take the joint apart, glue and plug the hole in the tenon, and re-drill.

DRAWBORE IN TWO DIRECTIONS

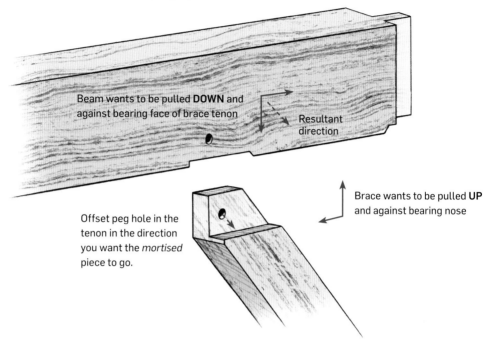

Beam wants to be pulled **DOWN** and against bearing face of brace tenon

Resultant direction

Brace wants to be pulled **UP** and against bearing nose

Offset peg hole in the tenon in the direction you want the *mortised* piece to go.

IDEAL DRAWBORE

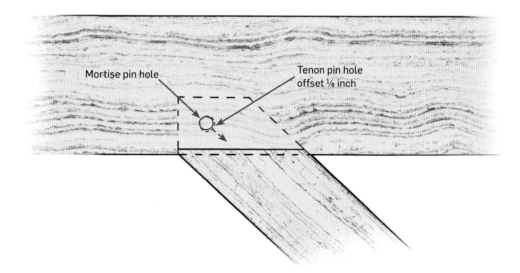

Mortise pin hole

Tenon pin hole offset ⅛ inch

Rules of Thumb for Joinery Design in Square Rule

Timber frame designers follow some key basic principles when designing joinery. In this book, much of the design work has been done for you (for example, lengths of tenons are given in the instructional text in chapter 6). However, it is important to understand the bigger picture of how a frame comes together, and these rules may come in handy if you choose to make variations on the core frame.

● **One of the main principles of all woodworking joinery design is to shape mortises and tenons so that each is parallel to the grain of its respective member.** Thus, tenon length should be a continuation of the grain out of the end of the timber, and not go off at an angle with what is called "short" grain. Mortise length should be oriented parallel to the grain (length) of the timber; once you've

severed that grain with one hole, it doesn't weaken the timber much to make more holes along that same line. As for all these "rules," there may be exceptions, but not without good reason.

● **Tenons have length, width, and thickness; mortises have depth (same as tenon length), length (same as tenon width), and width (same as tenon thickness).** Tenon width is usually the full width of the timber, and so the mating mortise is the same length and goes all the way across the housing. The exception here would be a mortise at the end of a timber, like sills and plates, where we leave 2 inches of relish so the mortise isn't open on the end. The tenon must then be cut back accordingly (as on the post illustrated at left).

TENON DIMENSIONS

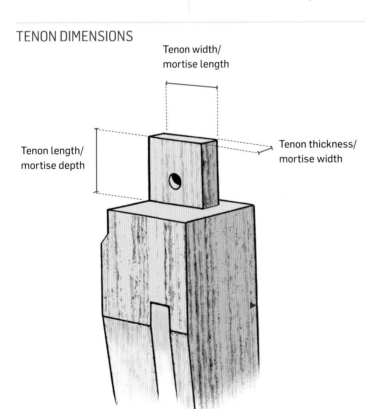

Tenon width/
mortise length

Tenon length/
mortise depth

Tenon thickness/
mortise width

➲ Mortises are arranged to allow drilling perpendicular to the surface of timber.
For example, the tenon on a brace coming in at an angle is "clipped" at 90 degrees to the shoulder so that the bearing end of the mortise can be square (See Laying Out Brace Mortises on page 94). You rarely see acute angles in mortises, as these are difficult to cut, but you may see obtuse ones (such as the non-bearing end of a brace mortise).

➲ Only tenoned members going into non-reference faces get reductions to the smaller perfect-timber-within. Housings, therefore, will be on the non-reference faces of mortised members. If a tenoned member is going into a reference face, then the tenoned timber's shoulder can be cut to the mortised timber's surface. An example of this would be the stub tenons on the bottoms of posts going into the reference faces (tops) of the sills. However, in some cases where aesthetics are an issue, it's desirable to make housings even on the reference face so that it looks the same as the opposite side. An example of this would be where braces and girts come into the posts from opposite sides.

➲ Mortise width (tenon thickness) should be about one-quarter the width of the mortised timber (in the smaller cross-sectional dimension), but not more than one-third. So 5- to 8-inch-thick timbers get mortises 1½ inches wide. We wouldn't consider 2-inch-wide mortises until our timbers get up to 8 inches or greater. In general, the benefit of a thicker tenon is not as great as the damage done by a wider mortise (which weakens the timber).

➲ **Tenon length is actually cut ⅛ inch under nominal, and mortises can be cut slightly deeper to avoid interference when the joint is assembled.** On post bottoms, tenons are nominally 2 inches long (1⅞ inches actual). These tenons are used to locate the posts and are not pinned; they are not meant to hold the frame down (gravity and nailed sheathing will do that). Tenons on post tops are 4 inches long (nominal). Tenons on braces, 4×5 wall girts, and door post tops are 3 inches long (nominal). Tenons on the center joist are 5 inches long (nominal).

➲ **All pin holes are centered on the width of the tenons and are 1½ inches off the shoulder, unless otherwise indicated.** Pin diameter is generally half the tenon thickness, so we use ¾-inch pins for 1½-inch-thick tenons. However, we go to 1-inch pins for larger tenons (longer or wider than 5 inches), even if they are still only 1½ inches thick. The only joinery that gets 1-inch pins in these frames are the sill tenons (5 inches long) and the through wedged half-dovetail on the tie beams. In any timber frame joint, pins should go into both mortise side walls at least as far as the tenon is thick. All of the pins in our frames here go all the way through the mortised timbers. In some cases, such as where plates and ties are at the same level, pins may hit another timber and not extend farther. In these instances, you have to move the centered pin location on the respective mortises and tenons to avoid the pins hitting each other. There is plenty of room to simply move them ¾ inch to the side in opposite directions.

PIN INTERFERENCE

These pegs will hit each other because they are centered on the same size tenon. To avoid this, offset the pegs ¾ inch in opposite directions.

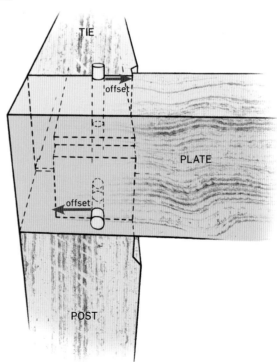

CHAPTER 6

THE TINY TIMBER FRAME

The 12 × 16-foot timber frame we will consider as the "core" project of this book is based on the garden shed designed by architect and timber framer Jack Sobon and described in his book *Timber Frame Construction*. We have made some variations in timber size and layout, but Jack's book makes a great reference to augment the instructions here. We'll first present the overall plan and sections of the frame showing relevant dimensions, along with a timber list. Then we will examine each piece of the frame and explain its joinery details.

Frame Specifications

The frames in this book are designed to certain spec-ifications that may differ depending on your location and access to timber. These specifications are:

→ **Timber species:** eastern white pine (*Pinus strobus*), Grade: No. 2 or better

DESIGN VALUES OF EASTERN WHITE PINE

→ **Fiber stress in bending (f_b):** 575 pounds per square inch (psi) (beams and stringers), 450 psi (posts and timbers)

→ **Shear parallel to the grain (f_v):** 125 psi

→ **Modulus of elasticity (E):** 900,000 psi

Species with similar or greater design values may be substituted in these designs. Design values for various northeastern species and measuring characteristics for grading can be found in NeLMA's *Standard Grading Rules for Northeastern Lumber* (see Resources).

LOADS

→ **Dead load:** 10 pounds per square foot (psf)

→ **Live load for ground floor:** 40 psf

→ **Live load for loft:** 30 psf

→ **Snow load (roof):** 50 psf

Plan Drawings

The first drawing of our core frame is an exploded view of the frame. This is useful for visualizing the timbers in the frame, which will help you avoid mistakes while working on your pieces on the sawhorses. It's the next best thing to building a model of the frame to work from. Note that we arbitrarily assigned a direction of view (from the southwest). This will, of course, differ depending on your building site, but it helps illustrate how to assign labels to the timbers based on their location. We gen-erally label from the north and west (this would also dictate ref-erence faces if not outside or top), but you can choose any system as long as you're consistent. (See page 53, Labeling the Frame.)

The next drawing, a plan view of the floor frame, looks straight down from overhead. One rule of drafting is to describe everything only once to keep the drawings cleaner; thus you'll find dimen-sions here that may not be found anywhere else. Later, if you're stumped on a timber's loca-tion, see if it is dimensioned on another drawing. This plan view shows the overall dimensions of the frame, the joist spacing, the distance from the outside of the

EXPLODED FRAME VIEW

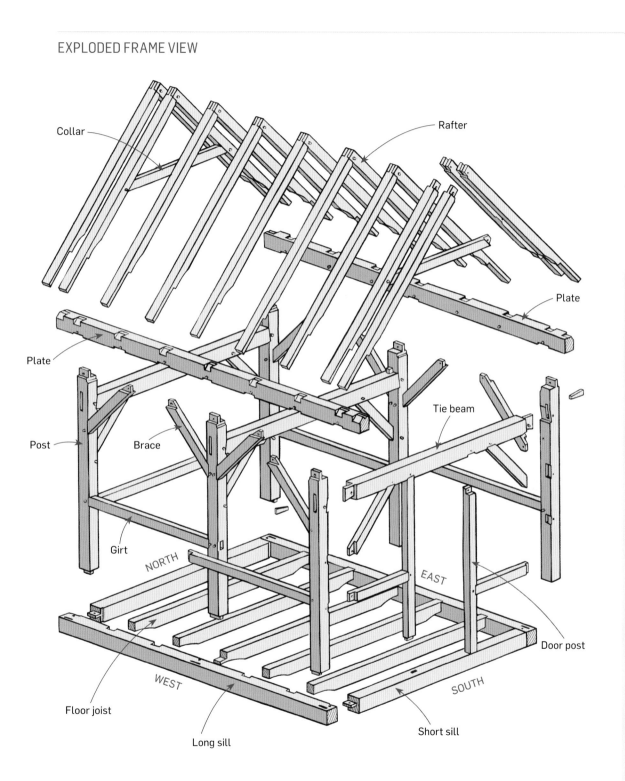

Collar

Rafter

Plate

Plate

Post

Brace

Tie beam

Girt

NORTH

EAST

Door post

WEST

Floor joist

Long sill

Short sill

SOUTH

long sills to the back of the joist pockets, and dimensions to the reference faces of the center posts and door posts. Note that the center bent is dimensioned to the north face of its timbers, and the door posts are dimensioned to the inside of the door opening. This indicates, then, the reference faces of those timbers. Mortises for the posts are also shown here. Section cutting planes A, B, 1, and 3, shown as dotted lines, are vertical slices through the building indicating the direction of view, toward walls A and B or bents 1 and 3, respectively.

The next four drawings are longitudinal and transverse sections. A section is a view from inside the building looking out in the direction indicated in the drawing title. We use sections here rather than elevations (views from outside the building) so that we can see the timbers better. The shaded boxes are timbers coming directly toward the viewer and represent the end grain. There are other timbers coming obliquely toward the viewer, such as braces and rafters, that aren't showing end grain and thus aren't shaded. The sections show other necessary dimensions, such as the heights to plates, tie beams, and wall girts; brace and rafter lengths; rafter spacing; roof pitch; and length of roof overhangs.

FLOOR PLAN

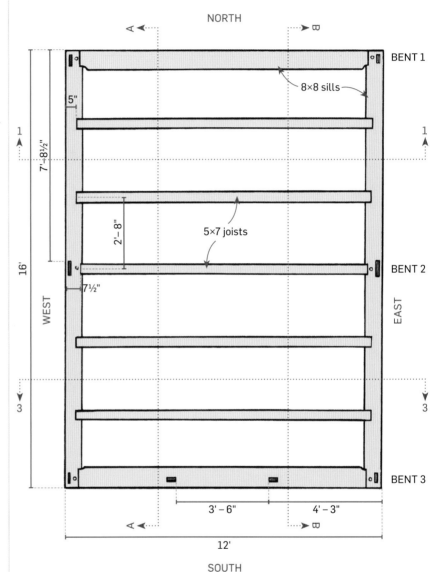

WEST LONGITUDINAL SECTION (SECTION A–A)

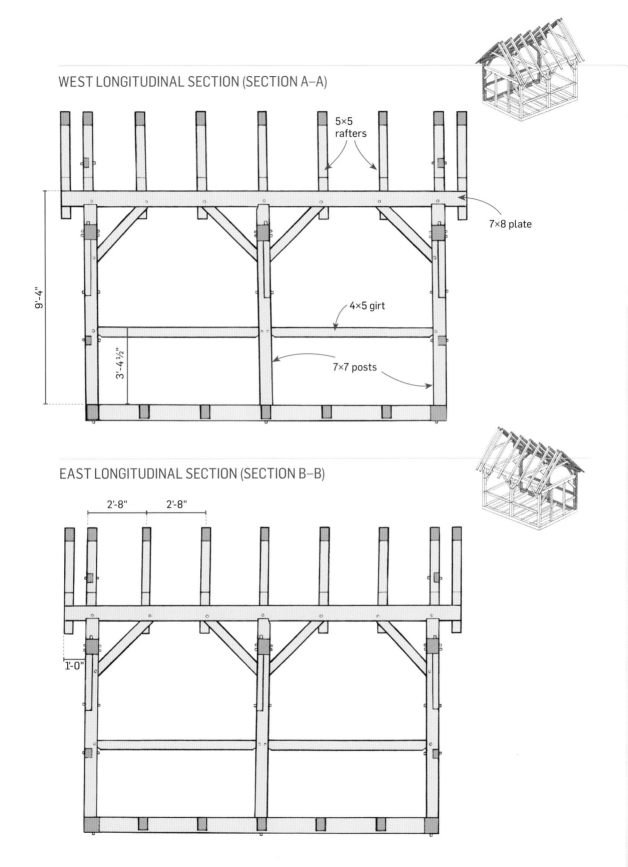

5×5 rafters

7×8 plate

4×5 girt

7×7 posts

9'-4"

3'-4½"

EAST LONGITUDINAL SECTION (SECTION B–B)

2'-8" 2'-8"

1'-0"

NORTH TRANSVERSE SECTION (SECTION 1–1)

ROOF PITCH:

12

12

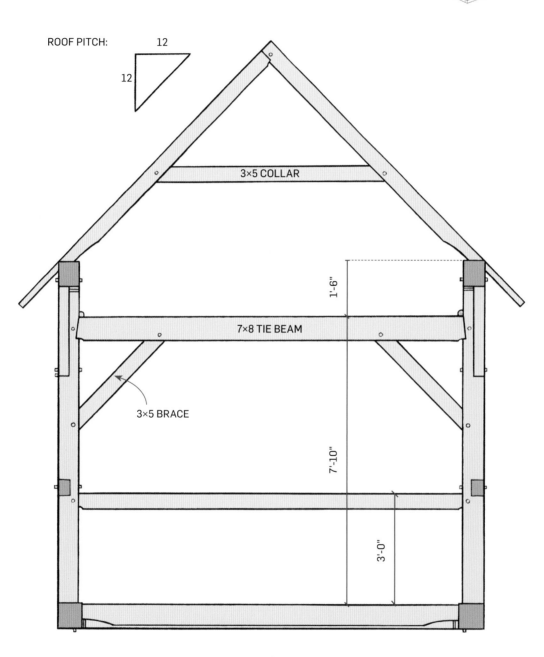

3×5 COLLAR

7×8 TIE BEAM

3×5 BRACE

1'-6"

7'-10"

3'-0"

SOUTH TRANSVERSE SECTION (SECTION 3–3)

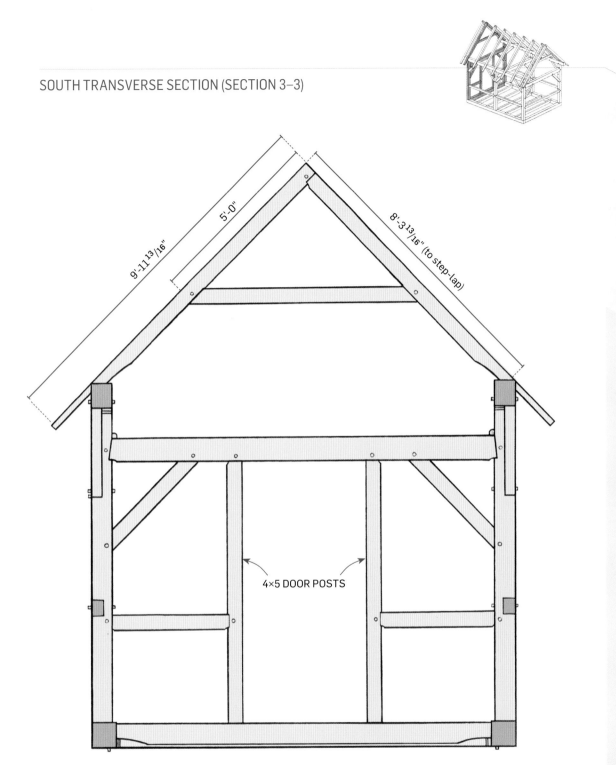

9'-11 13/16"

5'-0"

8'-3 13/16" (to step-lap)

4×5 DOOR POSTS

Timber List

The chart here provides you with a list of timbers needed for the core frame. Use it to order your timbers from a sawmill. Pins can be made by hand (see Making Pins on page 126) or ordered (see Resources).

Board footage (BF) is provided to help you estimate the weight of bents for raising: green eastern white pine weighs about 3 pounds per board foot. Calculate green oak at 6 pounds per board foot. Use the total BF figure to judge the capacity of a truck or trailer for shipping. The BF is calculated as follows:

BF = width (inches) × depth (inches) × length (feet) × quantity divided by 12.

Remember that one board foot equals the volume of wood in a board that's 12 inches square by 1 inch thick.

Now let's look at each piece in the frame, along with the joinery details. For pieces that are identical and interchangeable, only one piece will be considered. For pieces that are similar but with minor variations, we will explain the differences.

The first thing to determine for each piece is its shoulder-to-shoulder length. We will assume that no timber is more than ½ inch under nominal dimensions (over nominal is okay). Thus, we will frame ½ inch under nominal for our perfect-timber-within.

TIMBER LIST FOR THE CORE FRAME

TIMBER TYPE	NOMINAL (INCH) SIZE (WIDTH × DEPTH)	QUANTITY/ LENGTH (FEET)	BF (BOARD FOOTAGE)
Sills	8×8	2/12, 2/16	299
Tie beams	7×8	3/12	168
Plates	7×8	2/18	149
Posts	7×7	6/10	245
Joists	5×7	5/12	175
Rafters	5×5	18/10	375
Wall girts	4×5	5/8, 1/12	87
Door posts	4×5	2/8	27
Collars	3×5	2/10	25
Braces	3×5	7/10*	87.5
Total**			1637.5
Pins		12 1-inch dia., 75 ¾-inch	
Hardwood wedges	2¾ inch at wide end, tapered at ¾ inch in 8 inches	6/12"	Make wedges slightly narrower than 1½ inches

* Each 10-foot piece of brace stock will yield two braces.

** This total figure will help you to figure the weight of bents for raising, plus the total load for judging the capacity of a truck or trailer for shipping. Green eastern white pine weighs about 3 pounds per board foot; double that for green oak.

Sills

LONG SILLS

The two long sills are 16 feet long (final dimension) and have 10 mortises each. Two mortises on the ends are for the short sill's tenons. The three mortises in the top face are for the post bottom stub tenons, with their length laid out parallel to and 1½ inches off the outside reference face. Since these are mating with a reference face, no housing is required.

Like the mortises for the short sills, 2 inches of relish is left on the outside for the corner posts' tenons, but the center post tenons can be left at full width.

Here we learn an important concept: even though the post bottoms don't need to be reduced to go into a housing, since they land on a reference face, the width of the tenon itself needs to be reduced to the perfect-timber-within.

In the case of the posts, this would be 6½ inches from the reference face. When you are laying out these mortises, you don't know if the nominal 7-inch post is going to be 7 inches wide or 6⅞ inches wide or 7¼ inches wide, etc., but if you cut both the mortise and tenon to 6½ inches, you have it covered. Note on the plan that the center posts are dimensioned to their north side; this indicates the reference face of those posts and that the mortises for the bottom (and top) tenons of the post will start there (see center post top detail, lower drawing on page 96).

The remaining five mortises on the long sills are for the floor joists. Four of these are simple notches that the joists drop into, laid out 5 inches from the outside face.

The center joist is a *housed* mortise-and-tenon joint, as seen in the drawing, that serves as a tying joint to help hold the frame together until the flooring goes on and can actually help straighten out slight bows in the long sills. The joist pockets are laid out 32 inches on center; the first and last spaces are measured from the outside of the frame to the center of the first joist in.

Although square rule would dictate that we lay out from the north side of the joists and reduce each one to 4½ inches in width, that's a lot of work, so we will make our first exception to

LONG & SHORT SILLS

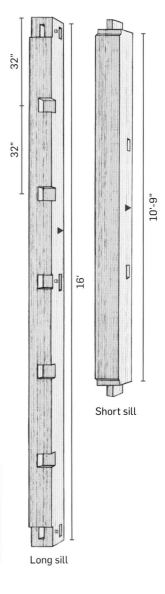

Short sill

Long sill

the rule here. When we have multiple interchangeable pieces, like joists and rafters, we will look at them and see how much they vary in width. For example, say our joists are all within ⅛ inch of a nominal 5 inches, with one at 5⅛ inches and the rest at 5 inches. Rather than reduce them all to 4½ inches, we would make all the pockets 5 inches wide and plane or spokeshave the one wide joist down to 5 inches. If only one was at 5 inches and the rest at 5⅛ inches, we would make all the pockets 5⅛ inches and let the narrow one be a little loose (flooring will hold it in). Once you have determined the width of the pockets, center them on the on-center layout lines.

Cut the sides of the drop-in joist pockets with a handsaw, then bore out the bulk of waste before paring the sides, bottom, and back. While the back of the drop-in joist pockets is not critical (the joists will be cut a bit short anyway for clearance), it is important that the bottoms be flat and at the correct depth so the joists have plenty of bearing surface and don't lie above or below the reference plane of the floor. Check often with your combination square set to 4½ inches.

SHORT SILLS

The short sills get a shoulder-to-shoulder length of 10 feet 9 inches (12 feet minus 7½ inches for each of the long sills). Nominal 5-inch tenons (actually 4⅞ inches long) will get added to this length during layout (but remember: it's the shoulder-to-shoulder length that is critical). The north sill in Bent 1 gets a tenon and reduction on each end; the south sill in Bent 3 gets these and also mortises for the stub tenons on the door posts. These are laid out like the other post tenons: length parallel to and 1½ inches off the outside reference face, and nominally 2 inches deep. The reference faces for the door posts are the outside face and the inside of the door opening, as shown by the dimensions in the plan view of the floor frame. The door posts are nominally 5 inches wide, so the mortises will be 4½ inches long, with one end on the reference line. Again, there is no housing required because this is going into a reference face.

When you are finished, label the sills. *A final note:* The sills are 8×8 for more than just structural reasons. They are 1 inch larger than the posts so there is a shelf around the base of the posts to support the flooring.

JOIST JOINERY

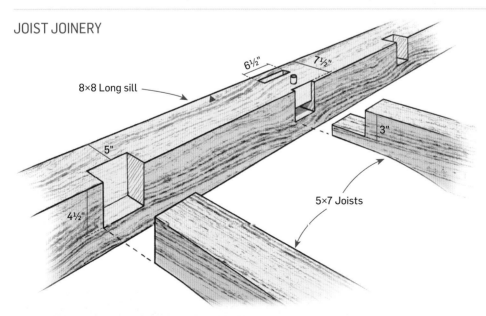

8×8 Long sill

6½"   7½"

5"

4½"

3"

5×7 Joists

JOIST POCKET LAYOUT AND CUTTING

1 From the control point, measure out to the sides of each pocket and transfer lines 4½ inches down the inside face of the sill.

2 On the top of the sill, measure in 5 inches from the arris to mark the backs of the pockets of the drop-in joists. (Measure in 7½ inches for the housing of the center joist.)

3 Cut the side of the pocket from corner to corner to sever the end grain as much as possible.

4 Bore out the back of the pocket from the top surface, being careful not to drill too deep, since the bottom is a bearing surface for the joist.

5 Chisel out the remaining material.

6 Check the squareness of the sides and the depth with your combination square.

Joists

The drop-in joists have a square cut on their ends (no tenon with shoulder), and their end-to-end length is 11 feet 1¾ inches (12 feet minus 5 inches minus 5 inches — and take off an additional ⅛ inch at each end to avoid interference in the back of the pocket).

The ends of the joists are reduced to a height of 4½ inches as measured from the top reference face. This reduction is carried out straight for 4 inches to clear the inside face of the sill, then gradually curved over the next 10 to 12 inches to return the joist to full depth (7 inches). This is done for structural reasons: if the pocket were deeper, it could unduly weaken the sill. The bending stress in the joist is greatest out in the middle, and so we can reduce its ends without compromising strength. This reduction is gradual so as not to concentrate shear stress (which is greatest at the ends) in one spot, which would be the case with a sharp-cornered notch. While this stress can be reduced adequately with just a 45-degree notch, by curving the reduction we distribute the stress even more.

This curve can be made with a bandsaw or a frame saw (a narrow, flexible blade in a rectangular frame, sort of like a big coping saw). However, using an axe and adze is much quicker, and the curve can be completed with a spokeshave if you want a smooth, finished appearance (for loft joists, for example, which are visible — for joists in the sills, probably not). You can lay out the curve by making and using a template that matches the curve of your adze.

The center joist is the same length as the short sills, as are its tenons (4⅞ inches). These tenons are barefaced, which means that the tenon is flush to one side, rather than having a shoulder on both sides. In this case, since it is flush to the underside of the joist, it is also known as a soffit tenon. Remember that when you taper the tenons on the sills and joists, only do it on the nonbearing surface (top) and sides — not the bottom, which should be kept exactly 4½ inches from the top of the joist for its entire length. Use your framing square to check.

Since the drop-in joists are interchangeable, and there is only one center joist with tenons, they don't need to be labeled.

DROP-IN & CENTER JOISTS

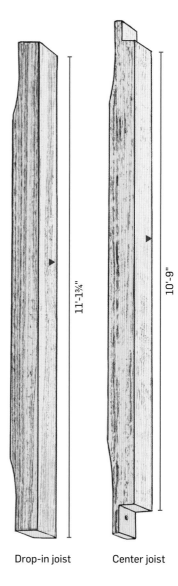

Drop-in joist Center joist

JOIST CUTTING

1 Remove most of the wood with an axe or saw.

2 Get closer to the line with a finer tool: the adze. Use it to trim the edges as close to the line as possible.

3 Leave the final four inches of the joist straight and level so it sits snugly in the pocket.

4 Use a spokeshave to bevel the sides of the joint down exactly to the line. This will give you a visual guide as you finish the rest of the surface.

5 Do the final paring with your spokeshave until the bevels on the edges disappear. Remember, this is a bearing surface, so accuracy is important.

6 The finished joint is a pleasure to feel and look at — if your spokeshave is sharp. It's best to have clear, knot-free wood in this area.

Posts

The posts may not be the pieces with the most joinery, but they have the most variety, with the tie beam, brace, and girt mortises, plus tenons on each end.

The shoulder-to-shoulder length is 8 feet 8½ inches, found by taking the height from the floor to the top of the plate (9 feet 4 inches) and subtracting the perfect-timber-within height of the plate (7½ inches). During layout, add 1⅞ inches for the stub tenon and 3⅞ inches for the top tenon.

The stub tenons on the bottoms should mirror the mortises made in the sills; the top tenons should as well, except they will be longer. Also, if the plates overhang the corner posts, as shown in the design (this is optional), then there is no reason to provide relish for the top mortise — the tenons on the corner posts can be the full width of the reduced post top, just like the center posts. You can taper all four faces of these tenons, as none of them are bearing.

The stub tenons don't get pinned, since gravity and wall sheathing will hold the building down. However, if your frame will remain open with only the roof covered, then you should make these tenons 4 inches long (nominal) and pin them. This requires lowering the sill tenons by 1 inch to avoid interference with the post bottom tenons. The pin holes on the top tenons are laid out 1½ inches off the shoulder and centered, and they are laid out on the face closer to the reference face of the timber. The tenon pins should be drawbored.

LAYING OUT BRACE MORTISES

All of the braces in our frame are "30-inch," which means that the brace forms the hypotenuse of a right triangle whose other legs are each 30 inches long (see page 108). These legs are measured according to the perfect-timber-within.

The mortises for the braces going from the posts to the plates and tie beams are laid out the same on all of the posts. Refer to the drawing opposite showing how the brace meets the post and transfer the measurements to your timber as follows: On the post, measure 30 inches down from the shoulder of the joint for the tie or plate, and make a mark. Measure across from the outer reference face and draw a

POST 3A

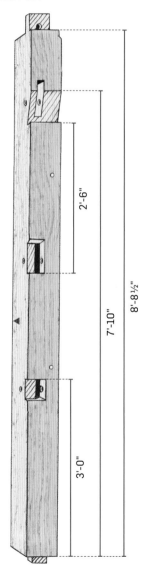

square line out to the opposite face representing the bearing nose of the brace. For nominal 7-inch wide posts, this line will extend 6½ inches in from the reference face (on the 8-inch-deep tie beams and plates, it will be 7½ inches down from the top surface of the beam/plate). Do not measure along the inside (non-reference) edge. Draw a line vertically along this perfect-timber-within, parallel to the reference face and back *toward* the joint you measured 30 inches from. It's easy here to mistakenly go the wrong way: remember 30 inches is to the *long* point of the brace. This line will be the length of the housing and represents the shoulder of the tenon.

The housings should be wide enough to accommodate the widest brace so that braces can be interchangeable. This is a departure from our usual square-rule practice of reducing tenoned pieces to a smaller consistent width; since there are so many braces in a typical frame, it saves a lot of work to make the housings a larger consistent width instead (see sidebar on page 111 for an alternative method). This will leave a slight gap where there

BRACE MORTISE LAYOUT

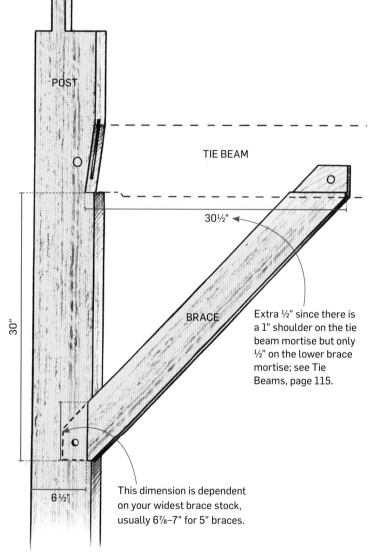

POST

TIE BEAM

30½"

30"

BRACE

6½"

Extra ½" since there is a 1" shoulder on the tie beam mortise but only ½" on the lower brace mortise; see Tie Beams, page 115.

This dimension is dependent on your widest brace stock, usually 6⅞–7" for 5" braces.

COMBINATION SQUARE WITH BRACE MORTISE LAYOUT

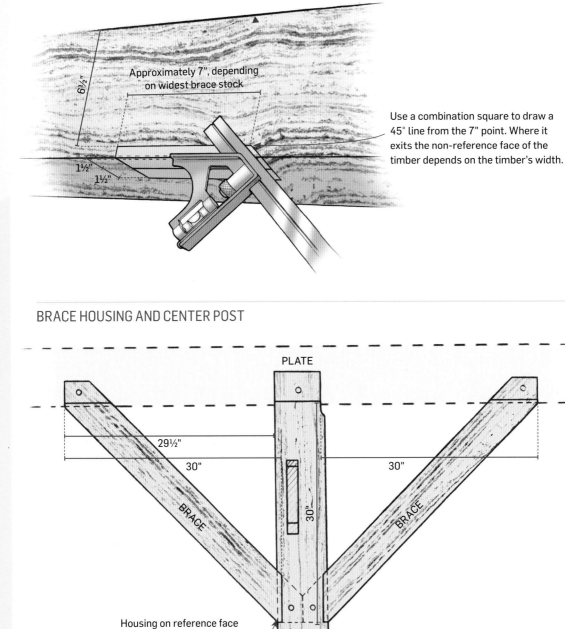

6½"

Approximately 7", depending on widest brace stock

1½"

1½"

Use a combination square to draw a 45° line from the 7" point. Where it exits the non-reference face of the timber depends on the timber's width.

BRACE HOUSING AND CENTER POST

PLATE

29½"

30"

30"

30"

BRACE

BRACE

Housing on reference face is measured in a true ½"

CENTER POST 2A

▶ = Symbol indicating arris of reference faces

are narrower braces, but since it is not a bearing point, it is only a cosmetic quirk of square rule. Do a trial brace layout on your widest brace stock to find the length; on 5-inch timber it is usually around 6⅞ to 7 inches (see Brace Mortise Layout, page 95). Use the 45-degree fence on your combination square to draw the line from this point out to the surface.

The outside faces of the braces will be flush to the outside reference faces of the posts, tie beams, and plates. Therefore, the housing for the brace is laid out on the adjacent face 3 inches in (from the outside reference face), with the inner 1½ inches being the mortise (the braces are nominally 3 inches wide). Don't draw these housing lines all the way across the inside face of the timber, or you might cut them by mistake. Although the upper end of the brace comes in at 45 degrees, you can bore the mortise in at 90 degrees all the way up to the point where the 45-degree portion of the housing starts. There will be a void there when the brace is installed, but it's a non-bearing surface and the damage along the grain below it has already been done. It's better not to take a chance in trying to get the angle right since that

may cause interference when inserting the brace.

Each long side of the frame has one brace that goes into the north reference face of each center post and extends up to the plate, and these need special consideration. Because the brace is going into a reference face, the brace housing in the post will be *measured in a true ½ inch*; girts going into that face will have housings of the same depth. Since the top of the post is not reduced on that side to ½ inch (although it could be), the brace layout on the plate as measured from the post housing needs to be adjusted to 29½ inches on that side, as we'll see later.

THE WEDGED HALF-DOVETAIL

The most complicated joint in the frame is the wedged half-dovetail for the connection between the tie beam and post. This is one of the strongest tension joints in timber framing, and is meant to resist the thrust of the roof in this design.

The dovetail mortise is a through mortise. To lay out this mortise on the post, find the control point that will be the top of the tie beam as dimensioned on the drawings (7 feet 10 inches from the bottom shoulder of the post) and mark it on the arris (you should have already done this when locating your joinery). Then put your

WEDGED HALF-DOVETAIL

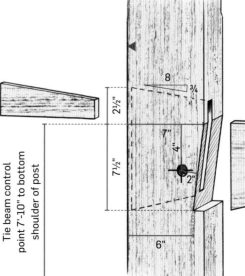
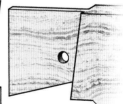

tape measure away and lay out the rest of this joint using your framing square.

1 Roll the timber so the reference face without the mortise is up (per the detail drawing). Holding 7½ inches on the control point with the framing square on the arris, mark the arris to represent the bottom of the reduced tie beam, then carry that point across to the inside face of the post (don't draw a line that won't be cut). Without moving the square, **mark the bearing shoulder of the tie beam.** This is nominally a 1-inch shoulder but is measured 6 inches from the arris, since you don't want to measure back from a non-reference face.

2 Go back up to the control point and **transfer with the framing square a point 7 inches toward the inside of the timber** (2a). Although your timber is nominally 7 inches wide, this point will be on the side if the timber is wider, or may actually be off the face if the timber is narrower than 7 inches. Regardless, 7 inches will be on your framing square.

Connect this point to the 6-inches mark made in step 1 to draw the diminished housing of the joint (2b). (If the timber is narrower, this line will exit the inside edge of the timber below the 7-inch point. If the timber is wider than 7 inches, you'll extend the line and it will exit further up the timber.)

3 Square all of the arris points down across the back reference face (one of the faces the mortise will be on). Then lay out the housing on the opposite face in exactly the same way as above. **Connect the corresponding points across the inside non-reference face** (one of the faces the mortise will be on). If that inside face is out of square, the line indicating the top of the housing will be sloping, but when you cut the housing, its face will be square to the reference face. This is a difficult concept to visualize, and contributes to the dovetail being the most complicated joint in the frame. We can summarize it thusly: *Any sloping line exiting onto an unsquare face will result in a sloping line across that face to meet the corresponding layout on the opposite side. (See detail 1 at right.)*

3

DOVETAIL MORTISE DETAIL 1

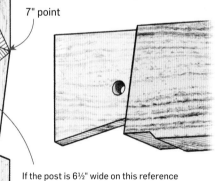

If the post is 7½" wide on this reference face and 7" on the opposite face, the housing line will exit the face of the timber here and slope downward across the inside face when connected to the exit point on the opposite face. The housing table, when cut, will be parallel to the reference plane.

If the inside non-reference face is square to this reference face, the housing line will exit here and continue square across.

7" point

If the post is 6½" wide on this reference face and 7" on the opposite, the housing line will exit the face of the timber here and slope upward across the inside face when connected to the exit point on the opposite face. The housing table, when cut, will be parallel to the reference plane.

4 Next, find a point along the diminished housing 6 inches down from a line squared across the timber from the control point. **This is done by holding the framing square with 6 inches on the arris control point and marking where the tongue intersects the housing line (4a). Connect this point to the lower 7½-inch point on the arris** that represents the bottom of the tenon, and this will show the bottom slope of the half-dovetail (4b). Since this line will not be cut on this face, mark it lightly with a dashed line that you can erase or plane it off later. Extend the line out to the inside edge of the timber. Again, lay out the opposite face in the same way, and **connect the corresponding points across the inside face of the timber (4c).** This line represents the bottom of the mortise. Remember that this will not be a square line if the inside face is out of square, so you can't just drop a square line down the inside face. (See detail 2 on the opposite page.)

6"

4a

4b

4c

DOVETAIL MORTISE DETAIL 2

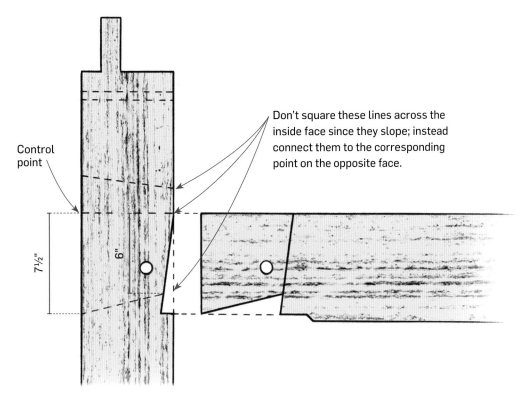

Control point

7½"

6"

Don't square these lines across the inside face since they slope; instead connect them to the corresponding point on the opposite face.

5 To lay out the mortise for the wedge that goes above the tie beam, **mark a point 2½ inches up from the control point** on the arris.

2½"

5

6 From this point, **lightly draw across the timber a dashed line with a slope of ¾ inch in 8 inches.** You can do this by holding the framing square with those two numbers on the arris. As with the other two sloping lines in this layout, the point at which the line exits the inside edge depends on how square (or not) the timber is.

6

7 **Transfer the line across the inside face** of the timber to the corresponding point on the opposite layout, and you will have the top of the mortise.

7

8 **Draw the mortise** 1½ inches wide, 1½ inches off the reference face.

8

CUTTING THE DOVETAIL MORTISE

Be sure to double- and triple-check your layout of this complicated joint before cutting.

1 Since both the top and bottom of this mortise are sloped to form the dovetail and go all the way through, you will need to **drill a ½ inch or so more than halfway from either side.** On the backside, start drilling far enough in from the end of the mortise to avoid drilling into the slope. This assumes you're drilling perpendicular to the face. Although it's possible to tip your drill to follow the slope, it is easier to drill square and then chisel to the slope using the dashed line you drew on the side as a guide.

2 **Use your framing square to check the slope** inside the mortise; when its straight edge just touches your top and bottom layout lines on both faces, without too much undercutting in between, you're there. Check for width by making sure the 1½-inch tongue of the square goes through the mortise everywhere.

3 Cut to depth the bottom shoulder line across the inside face of the timber. After the mortise is completely done you can **use your chisel to remove the diminished housing,** dishing it out slightly for shrinkage.

4 **Lay out the pin hole** 2 inches off the housing and 4 inches down from the control point (as shown on page 97); this is a 1-inch-diameter pin.

5 As one final detail, take your chisel and **remove about a ¼-inch bevel from the top of the mortise** where the wedge will exit on the inside. Otherwise, because the mortise is sloped down to this point, when you drive the wedge it can split out the wood on the inside.

2

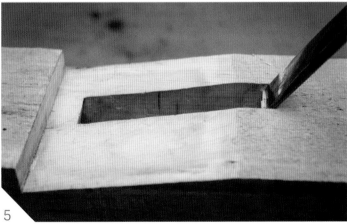

5

MAKING THE WEDGE

The drawing below shows the dimensions of the hardwood wedge that secures the wedged half-dovetail joint. To make it, first cut out a pattern from a piece of ¼-inch plywood (cut with a jigsaw or bandsaw) or heavy poster board. Then, see if you can find enough scrap hardwood blocks to make six 12-inch-long wedges. If you don't have scraps lying around your shop, go to a sawmill and ask if they'll cut off a few feet of hardwood lumber for you. Millwork shops and furniture makers may also have short scraps they'll give to you or sell cheaply.

The first step is to plane the blocks down to slightly less ($\frac{1}{32}$ inch or so) than 1½ inch in thickness. I use a thickness planer, but a jointer or hand plane can work as well. You don't want to have to force the wedge in and possibly split the top of the post. Once you've planed the blocks, lay your pattern on each piece and draw the slope of the wedge. With such short pieces, cutting is best done on a bandsaw, although a tapering jig can be made for a table saw. A handsaw can also be used if you are able to secure the pieces down while cutting or can cut them from longer stock. An electric jigsaw usually doesn't work well on 1½-inch-thick hardwood as the blade will want to drift.

Once the wedges are cut, clean up the saw marks and any variations with a sander or jointer, and lightly chamfer the edges and ends with a block plane.

When assembled, the wedge on this joint will extend a few inches from the outside face of the post. Give the wedge a final few taps and cut it off before putting the siding on.

GIRT AND BRACE MORTISES

The rest of the layout on the posts is for brace and girt mortises, which will mirror the tenons. Using the dimensions in the plans, find the control points along the arris, and transfer the marks across to the appropriate face. The brace and girt housings on the non-reference faces of the post get framed to 6½ inches from the opposite reference face, but if there are housings on a reference face (as on the north face of Bent 2 center posts), those go into the reference face a true ½ inch (see Barefaced Housings and Tenons in Reference Faces on page 106).

Note that the girt heights are offset on adjacent sides of the building; this is to avoid any interference between the tenons and pins as the frame is assembled.

DOVETAIL WEDGE

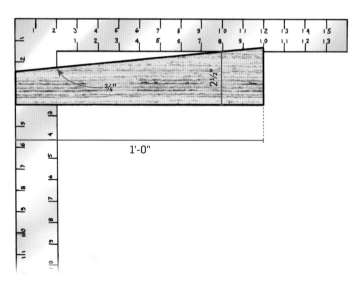

Girts

First let's find the shoulder-to-shoulder length of the girt in the north bent (Bent 1). Take a look at the plan view again on page 84. The dimension to the outside reference faces of the posts is 12 feet. The girt is framed to the perfect-timber-within, or 6½ inches in from each end, so the shoulder-to-shoulder length is 10 feet 11 inches.

The four girts in the longitudinal walls conveniently end up being the same length. From the north reference face of Bent 1 to the reference face of Bent 2, the dimension shown is 7 feet 8½ inches (this nominally centers a 7-inch post in the frame). The girts between these bents are framed 6½ inches in from the reference face of Bent 1 but go ½ inch into the reference face of Bent 2, as explained in Barefaced Tenons and Housings in Reference Faces (page 106). Thus, the shoulder-to-shoulder length is 7 feet 8½ inches minus 6½ inches plus ½ inch, for a total of 7 feet 2½ inches. The dimension from the north reference face of Bent 2 to the south (outside) reference face of Bent 3 is 8 feet 3½ inches

(16 feet minus 7 feet 8½ inches). The girts between these bents are framed 6½ inches in from the reference face of Bent 2 and 6½ inches in from the reference face of Bent 3. Thus, the shoulder-to-shoulder length is 8 feet 3½ inches minus 13 inches, or . . . 7 feet 2½ inches. So all four of these girts are interchangeable and don't need to be labeled.

The last girts to consider are the two in Bent 3 going into the door posts. We are given the dimension from the outside of the bent to the inside of the door opening: 4 feet 3 inches. Subtract 6½ inches for the corner post and 4½ inches for the door post to get a shoulder-to-shoulder length for the door girts of 3 feet 4 inches.

All girt tenons are a nominal 3 inches (2⅞ inches, actual) in length. Refer to Barefaced Tenons and Housings in Reference Faces (page 106) to determine whether to make them barefaced or not.

GIRT (BENT 1)

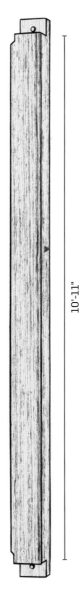

10'-11"

Barefaced Tenons and Housings in Reference Faces

Girts are any horizontal timbers going between posts, but here we'll use the term for the 4×5 minor members used as siding nailers, window sills, and handy shelves for knickknacks. They also help hold the frame together during the raising. Girts sometimes go into members larger than themselves, such as the 7×7 posts, but they also go into some that are the same size, such as the 4×5 door posts.

Different tenon types are used for different situations. As with a brace, we use a *barefaced* tenon when the girt goes into a larger member; this avoids having to cut two shoulders on the tenon and a second housing table beyond the mortise on the post, thus saving considerable work. We can't use a barefaced tenon where the girt goes into a post of the same width (like the door posts) because this would result in an open mortise on the inside of the post. In this case, we lay out the tenon 1½ inches off the reference face. Although we still have to cut a second shoulder on the tenon, the second housing table on the post is easier because it can be accessed from the inside.

Assuming all of the girts are at least 4×5 inches, barefacing then means that the 1½-inch-thick tenons will be laid out 2½ inches off the reference face. Girts that are wider than 4 inches will need to be shaved down on their inside face to go into the housing, just like thicker braces are shaved down to 3 inches. The vertical height of the girts is reduced to 4½ inches where they enter the receiving (mortised) members, following our square rule method. As with all the other reductions, bring the reduction out 1½ inches from the shoulder to clear the inside faces of the posts.

Using braces and girts with barefaced tenons assumes that the stock is of nominal thickness or greater, and that you will only have to shave them down a little. This saves having to do a major reduction on both the faces opposite the reference faces (bottom and inside for girts), which is more work and looks odd. You can ask your sawyer to provide timber at nominal or greater, and a good one can usually accommodate this. If a few are under nominal in thickness, you'll have to do something to account for this so they aren't too loose in the mortise. If you have extra timber, perhaps you can reject the ones that are undersized. Or you can map the offending joint and make the housing and/or mortise narrower to match the tenoned piece. In any case, you want to lay out the joint so that the reference faces are flush if they are on the outside of the building.

On the center posts, girts and braces come into both reference (north in this case) and non-reference faces. Earlier we had a rule of thumb that we are now going to break: Only tenoned members going into non-reference faces get reductions to the smaller perfect-timber-within, and thus the housings will be on the non-reference faces of mortised members. However, it looks odd and unsymmetrical to have braces and girts sticking out different amounts on opposite sides of the posts, so we will opt to house the braces and girts going into layout faces a true ½ inch. This makes them look symmetrical but will cause one minor complication when we lay out the plates, as we'll see later. Alternatively, you can opt not to cut housings in the layout faces, as true square rule would dictate, with no structural consequences and some aesthetic ones. You just need to account for the decision in your layout,

WHEN TO BAREFACE

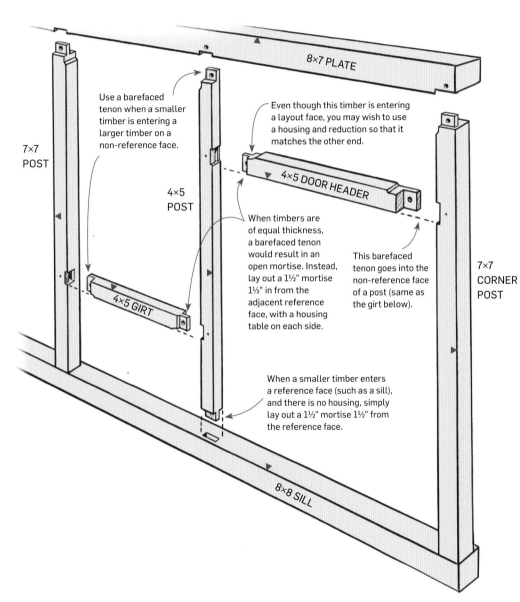

8×7 PLATE

7×7 POST

Use a barefaced tenon when a smaller timber is entering a larger timber on a non-reference face.

4×5 POST

Even though this timber is entering a layout face, you may wish to use a housing and reduction so that it matches the other end.

4×5 DOOR HEADER

When timbers are of equal thickness, a barefaced tenon would result in an open mortise. Instead, lay out a 1½" mortise 1½" in from the adjacent reference face, with a housing table on each side.

This barefaced tenon goes into the non-reference face of a post (same as the girt below).

7×7 CORNER POST

4×5 GIRT

When a smaller timber enters a reference face (such as a sill), and there is no housing, simply lay out a 1½" mortise 1½" from the reference face.

8×8 SILL

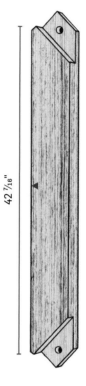

Braces

Braces are interchangeable and one of the most common and important members in the frame. They provide strength to resist racking, and they ensure the frame stands plumb and square when erected on a level foundation. Thus, the accuracy of layout is critical; if a brace is even ⅛ inch too short or too long, the frame may not go together. Braces are the shortest pieces in the frame and can be cut inside on a rainy day, if need be.

Our core frame calls for "30-inch" braces. Remember that this is the leg length of the right triangle, not the actual hypotenuse length that the brace forms. Braces can be longer, which is usually better for racking strength, but then they can get in the way of windows and decrease headroom inside. Braces 36 inches long are common, and 24 inches is the minimum.

BRACE

42 ⁷/₁₆"

BRACE LENGTH

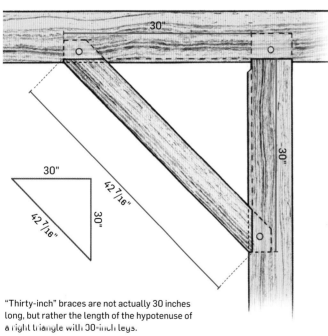

30"

30"

42 ⁷/₁₆"

30"

30"

42 ⁷/₁₆"

30"

"Thirty-inch" braces are not actually 30 inches long, but rather the length of the hypotenuse of a right triangle with 30-inch legs.

Here is the procedure for laying out a brace:

1 On the 5-inch-wide layout face of a 3×5 timber at least 5 feet long, lay out the brace's shoulder-to-shoulder length of 42⁷⁄₁₆ inches; this is the hypotenuse of a 30-inch right triangle. Leave enough length at each end for tenons (about 6 inches) and avoid knots in these areas. Note that the long bottom edge of the brace is the reference arris.

2 Measure in ³⁄₈ inch (for a ½-inch nominal housing) from the 3-inch layout face along the lines drawn in Step 1. ³⁄₈ inch is the leg length of a triangle when the hypotenuse is ½ inch (nominal housing depth).

3 Use your framing square as shown to draw 45-degree lines in both directions from the arris through the intersection drawn in Step 2. Line 1 is the shoulder of the brace tenon, and Line 2 is the bearing surface of the tenon.

4 Measure 2⁷⁄₈ inches (for a 3-inch nominal tenon) from Line 1 along Line 2 and strike a 45-degree line parallel to Line 1. This line (Line 3) is the end of the tenon.

BRACE LAYOUT STEP 1

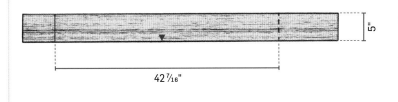

42⁷⁄₁₆"

5"

BRACE LAYOUT STEP 2

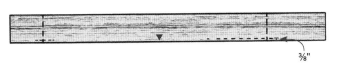

³⁄₈"

BRACE LAYOUT STEP 3

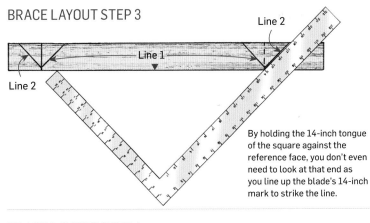

Line 2

Line 1

Line 2

By holding the 14-inch tongue of the square against the reference face, you don't even need to look at that end as you line up the blade's 14-inch mark to strike the line.

BRACE LAYOUT STEP 4

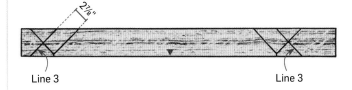

2⁷⁄₈"

Line 3

Line 3

5 Cut Line 3 first, as it's the least critical, then cut Line 2 (more critical). Don't cut Line 1 until you've laid out the tenon lines on the newly cut ends. The shoulder cut of Line 1 is only 1½ inches deep.

6 Remove waste (shaded area) by cutting 1½ inches deep along Line 1 and chiseling or rip-sawing from the end.

7 Lay out the pin hole 1½ inches off the shoulder and 2 inches from the bearing face; this makes it approximately centered on the tenon. Because the brace runs at an angle, the drawbore will be in two directions: up the axis of the brace and toward the shoulder a light ⅛ inch.

8 If the brace stock is thicker than 3 inches, spokeshave or plane the inside non-reference face until it is 3 inches thick, at least far enough down to clear the mortised timber housing.

9 Taper the cheeks (broad sides) of the tenon, but not the bearing face, and chamfer the end.

BRACE LAYOUT STEP 5

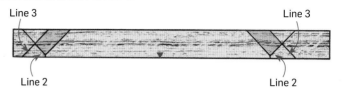

Line 3 Line 3
Line 2 Line 2

BRACE LAYOUT STEP 6

3" 1½"

BRACE LAYOUT STEP 7

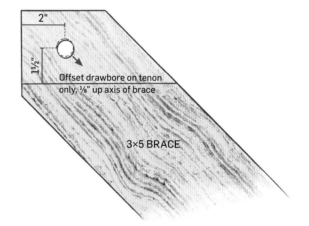

2"

1½"

Offset drawbore on tenon only, ⅛" up axis of brace

3×5 BRACE

Alternative Brace Layout

The layout of the brace (and collar tie) joints may seem odd, especially after the frame is assembled and you see a slight gap at the non-bearing end of the housing to accommodate the widest possible brace. Why do we do it this way?

There are a number of different methods that today's timber framers use to lay out braces. Our method is a nod to the historical one in which framers used a variety of sizes of timber to make braces — whatever was left over as the frame neared completion. Rather than take the time to mill up a bunch of 3×5s, traditional framers might use stock that was meant for girts, joists, or other members. Thus, they would make all the mortises wide enough to accept not only 5-inch-wide braces but also ones that might be 6 or 8 inches wide. In old square-ruled buildings you will indeed see brace mortises that are sometimes 2 to 3 inches wider than the brace going into them.

This method saved material and labor. In our frames today we can easily get brace timbers milled for 3×5 braces, so the variation will be slight. Therefore, any gaps created by the larger housings will be small as well, accommodating any out-of-squareness or difference in width in the non-reference (short) side of the brace.

If you don't want to see any gap, it is possible to lay out the braces from the short side, making the inside of the brace the reference face. The lengths of the legs (30 inches) and hypotenuse (42 7/16 inches) then become the inner dimensions of the triangle instead of the outer dimensions, requiring the braces to be longer. The 5-foot-long rough stock should still work, but you will have less room to play with for avoiding knots and other defects.

The housings for braces laid out this way will be exactly 6 9/16 inches long (the hypotenuse of a 4 5/8 × 4 5/8-inch triangle). Any variations in the width or squareness of the brace would be visible at the nosing on the long face: it would stick out of or be recessed into the housing.

This alternative method is shown in the accompanying drawing. We prefer to lay out from the bearing (long) side of the brace, however, and describe that method throughout this book.

ALTERNATIVE BRACE LAYOUT

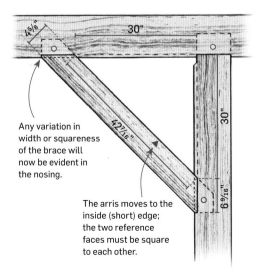

4 5/8"   30"

42 7/16 "

30"

6 9/16 "

Any variation in width or squareness of the brace will now be evident in the nosing.

The arris moves to the inside (short) edge; the two reference faces must be square to each other.

Collars

Collars connect the two pairs of rafters at the gable ends and are used as nailers for siding. You can also frame a small window in above them. Some may call these collar "ties" but that implies that they keep the rafters from spreading due to roof load. In reality, that job is handled by the rafter seats in the plate as well as the tie beams below. A horizontal member between the rafters doesn't provide significant tying unless it is right down at plate level. A collar up in the middle of the rafter span does help keep them from sagging under snow load, however, and provides some bracing in the roof to resist lateral loads.

The collars are laid out just like a brace, only the point-to-point length is longer. To find that length, look at the south transverse section (page 87), which shows the rafter length. The collar layout drawing opposite shows that the dimension to the collar control point is 5 feet down from the peak, as measured along the top reference face of the rafter. Square this point down to the inside face of the rafter and measure 4½ inches in to locate the point in the housing that is the bearing nose of the collar.

Now we need to find the corresponding point at the peak that represents the perfect-timber-within junction of the two right angle legs of the triangle that the collar forms the hypotenuse of. Looking at the rafter peak detail, we see that point is 4½ inches in from both rafters' top surfaces. Therefore, the length of the triangle's right angle legs is 5 feet minus 4½ inches, or 4 feet 7½ inches. Using a calculator and the Pythagorean theorem ($a^2+b^2=c^2$), we find that the collar length is 6 feet 6½ inches; this corresponds to the length of 42$\frac{7}{16}$ inches for a 30-inch brace leg. Once you find that point, lay out the tenons and pin holes just like a brace (as with a brace, the bottom of the collar is the reference face).

COLLAR

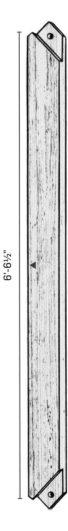

6'-6½"

COLLAR LAYOUT

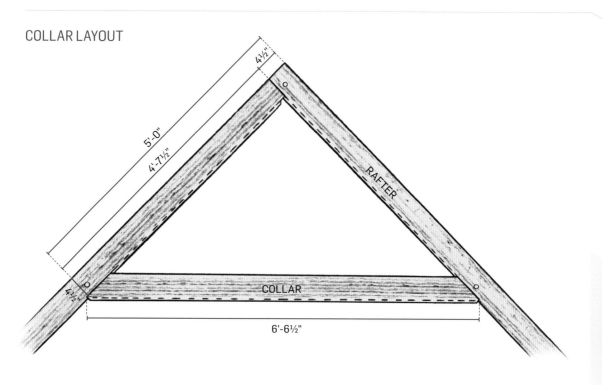

RAFTER PEAK DETAIL

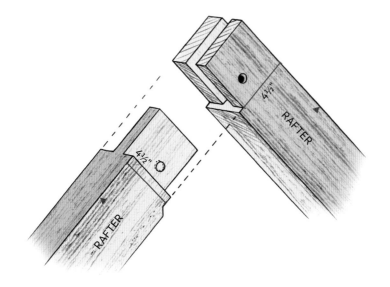

Door Posts

The door posts have their 5-inch width parallel to the bent direction so that their thickness (4 inches) is the same as the girts coming into them. The mortise and housing for those girts is a mirror of the girts' double-shouldered tenons.

The bottom of the door post goes into a reference face of the sill, so there is no housing, and the post will have a stub tenon laid out 1½ inches off the reference face. Even though the post itself is not reduced to go into a housing, this tenon, as with the other post bottoms, is cut back on the non-reference side to the perfect-timber-within, or 4½ inches.

The top tenon, since it is going into a non-reference face in the tie beam, will get a barefaced tenon 2½ inches in from the outside reference face, and the entire post top will be reduced to 4½ inches in width where it goes into the housing. The dimension given from the top of the sill to the top of the tie beam is 7 feet 10 inches. Subtract 7½ inches for the distance from the top of the tie beam to the housing for the door posts, and you get a shoulder-to-shoulder length of 7 feet 2½ inches.

DOOR POST

7'-2½"

3'

Tie Beams

The tie beams hold the walls together, with the wedged half-dovetail resisting the thrust from the rafters on the plate. The tie beam could also support loft joists, should you decide to include them (see chapter 7), and includes a nominal 1-inch shoulder at the bottom of the diminished housing to provide extra bearing capacity. The shoulder-to-shoulder length from the bottom corner of this shoulder, then, is 12 feet minus 6 inches minus 6 inches, or 11 feet even. The shoulder is also 7½ inches down from the top arris of the tie beam, since the top is the reference face and we are reducing the nominal 8 inch depth to a perfect 7½ inches.

The sloped shoulder of the diminished housing produces a point on the top arris of the tie exactly 7 inches in from the outside of the mating post, so you can also use this as a layout point; the shoulder-to-shoulder length there, at the top of the tie beam, is 10 feet 10 inches.

Once the shoulder is laid out, the tenon is fairly straightforward, being a mirror of the mortise layout on the post. Mark the tenon thickness (1½ inches),

and cut the cheeks, removing the material around the tenon before laying out and cutting the reduction or the dovetail. Use extra care cutting the shoulders and, especially, the bottom bearing surface of the joint — keep it square to the reference face for full contact. After the tenon is finished to thickness and the half-dovetail cut, take ¼ inch off the end so that when the post shrinks, the tenon won't stick out the back. Finally, lay out and drill the 1-inch pin hole, offsetting the bit slightly up and in to the shoulder so that you draw the mortised post in that direction, tightening the joint.

Brace mortises in the tie beams and plates are laid out the same way as described earlier with the posts, but their *location* is slightly different. Remember that you've created a 1-inch shoulder on the post for extra bearing, but the bottom of the brace only goes into a nominal ½-inch housing in the post. In order to keep the legs of the brace triangle square and 30 inches long, the control point for the brace on the tie beam must be located 30½ inches from the point at the bottom of

TIE BEAM 3AB

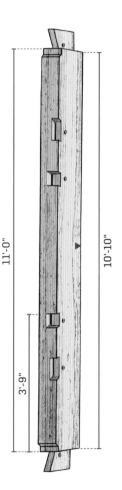

11'-0"

10'-10"

3'-9"

TIE BEAM LAYOUT DETAIL

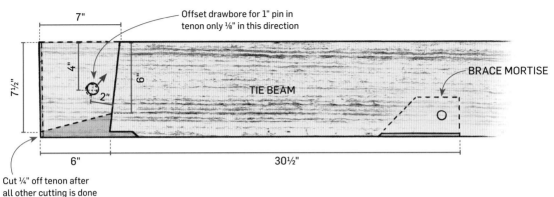

7"

Offset drawbore for 1" pin in
tenon only ⅛" in this direction

4"

7½"

6"

2"

BRACE MORTISE

TIE BEAM

6"

30½"

Cut ¼" off tenon after
all other cutting is done

the diminished housing. Another way of looking at this (perhaps less confusing) is that the end of the brace housing is 36½ inches from the outside of the building, since it's a 30-inch brace framed to a perfect-timber-within that is 6½ inches in from the reference face. (See Brace Mortise Layout on page 95).

If you stick with the original plans and put your door in the gable end wall, you will have housings and mortises for the door posts in the bottom of the tie beam. Alternatively, you can move the door and cut longer door posts to go into the underside of the plate. Layout will be the same; follow the guidelines for laying out barefaced tenons in non-reference faces (page 106).

THE TIE BEAMS AND PLATES ARE OFFSET 10 ½ INCHES ON THE POSTS. *This separates the joinery to avoid weakening the post in one spot, but the distance is still close enough for the wedged half-dovetail to efficiently resist the roof thrust on the plate. The distance between the tie beam and the plate should not exceed 2 feet without changing the post size (see Chapter 7).*

Plates

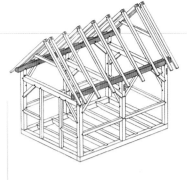

The plates are the longest pieces in the frame and also have the most joinery: all mortises and rafter pockets. The design includes a 12-inch overhang on each gable end of the building that helps protect the siding, but if you have trouble getting timbers longer than 16 feet, you could cut the plates flush to the outside of the structure and then frame the overhang with lumber after the sheathing goes on. This would also keep the timber from penetrating the insulated envelope of the building, a good idea in cold climates. The water vapor in warm, moist air escaping to the outside could condense when it hits the dew point, potentially causing rot over time. The same issue concerns the rafter tails, which could also be cut flush to the exterior and the overhang at the eaves formed with the roof insulation system (see chapter 9).

The plates are 18 feet long, end to end, and the mortises and housings on the bottom (non-reference) face are mirrors of the post tops described earlier. The housings are laid out 7½ inches down from the top, and the center housings are 6½ inches wide, starting at 7 feet 8½ inches from the north side of Bent I.

If you look carefully at the longitudinal sections, you'll see that the south (non-reference) faces of the center posts are reduced to go into the plates, while the north face is not because it's the reference face (also see brace housing detail on page 96). This follows the square rule, but it requires a brace mortise layout adjustment similar to the one we had to make on the tie beam. The brace going into the plate and the north face of the post is housed a true ½ inch into the post, as explained earlier, but the post is not reduced at the top by ½ inch (although it could be if you wanted the extra work). So, again, in order to keep the legs of the brace triangle square and 30 inches long, the control point for the north brace in the plate must be located 29½ inches from the north shoulder of the housing.

These adjustments of the brace housings in the plate and tie beam are solely due to the fact that we are housing onto the layout face of the posts for aesthetic reasons to keep the braces and girts looking

PLATE

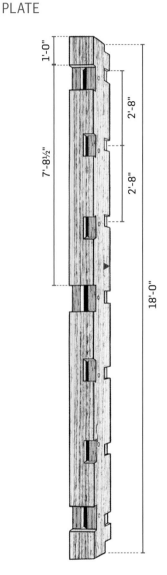

STEP-LAP RAFTER SEAT

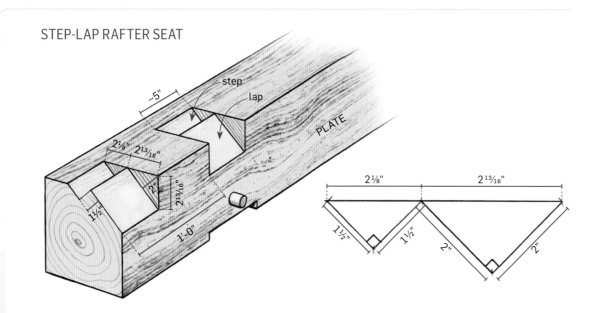

symmetrical. You don't need to house them for structural reasons, so if this seems too confusing, you can skip it. But I think visualizing these adjustments helps you learn the principles of square rule.

STEP-LAP RAFTER SEAT

The tops of the plates get one of the coolest joints in timber framing: the step-lap rafter seat. Since the rafters do not rest on a ridge beam or have ceiling joists holding their feet together (like in stick framing), there must be some way to transfer the thrust of the roof to the plates and carry it down the posts to let the tie beam handle it. The step in this joint is perpendicular to the axis

of the rafter and bears that thrust. The rafter tail continues out to form the eaves overhang, going through the "lap" part of the joint. The top surface of the rafter is flush with the arris of the plate (see Rafter Tail on page 124).

First, though, you need to locate the rafters on the top of the plate. Because there are lots of rafters it makes sense to measure their widths and make the pocket match the majority of them, like we did with the joists. A few that are wider can be shaved down, and ones slightly narrower can be a little loose. This saves the work of having to reduce down the whole lot of them by ½ inch under nominal, as per strict square rule.

Let's assume the rafters are all within ⅛ inch of 5 inches wide and make the pockets that width. There is one rafter at each end of the plates, so we can mark a short line for the inside of each end rafter 5 inches in from the end. There are also rafters 1 foot in from the ends of each plate, with their reference faces flush to the outside of the end bents; siding will be nailed to these faces and the collars. Mark those lines and an inside line at 5 inches. The centerlines of the remaining rafters are found by dividing up the 16 feet from outside to outside into 6 equal spaces, or 2 feet 8 inches each (like the joists). Measure out 2½ inches to each side of the centerlines to locate the sides of these interior rafters.

LAYING OUT THE STEP-LAP

To lay out the step-lap itself, extend the side lines in from the arris about 5 inches on the top and 3 inches down the outside layout face. The 2-inch depth of the lap and 1½-inch depth of the step are measured perpendicular to the roof pitch. The distances back and down from the arris for the lap is the hypotenuse of a 2-inch right triangle. On the top, you will find a second line, to the back of the step, that will be the length of the hypotenuse of a 1½-inch right triangle. We calculate those distances as $2^{13}/_{16}$ inches and $2^{1}/_{8}$ inches, respectively. These distances are only for a 12:12 pitched roof (45 degrees), and will be different if the roof pitch changes (see chapter 7).

USE YOUR COMBINATION SQUARE *riding along the arris to set out the lines marking the back of the lap and step, as well as the sides of the joint.*

A TRICK OF THE TRADE

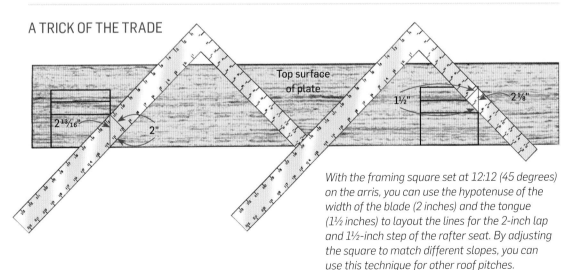

With the framing square set at 12:12 (45 degrees) on the arris, you can use the hypotenuse of the width of the blade (2 inches) and the tongue (1½ inches) to layout the lines for the 2-inch lap and 1½-inch step of the rafter seat. By adjusting the square to match different slopes, you can use this technique for other roof pitches.

CUTTING THE STEP AND LAP

 Carefully saw the side lines of the lap.

 Chop out the triangle of wood in between, finishing the lap entirely before starting the step. A small axe makes quick work of removing this material but requires some courage and control to avoid going too deep. It can also be roughed out with a chisel (2a). Complete the final paring with a chisel, in any case. A block of wood cut to the roof slope (45 degrees, in this case) can help guide your chisel here (2b) and in step 3.

1

2a

2b

3 To cut the step, **take your 1½-inch chisel and place its corner on the side line with the bevel facing into the waste.** Sight along the top edge of the chisel to line it up with the back line of the lap; this establishes the angle. You can also use an angled block of wood to help guide you. **Chop in partway with the chisel and mallet, and then go around and repeat the process from the other side,** alternating until your chisel reaches the bottom of the triangle. The 1½-inch chisel width can be used as a gauge, since that's how deep the step is.

4 **Chisel away the materials between the two side lines** of the step, being careful not to go too deep or deviate from the proper angle. Work your way down slowly and carefully, since these are both important bearing surfaces. Always sever the end grain with your chisel before paring out the material in between.

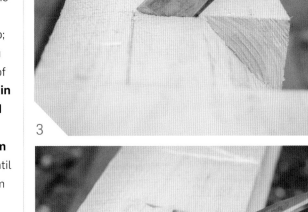

3

4a

4b

5 **Use your combination square on the face of the lap to check your work,** since the step is square to the lap. The joints on the ends are easier to cut because you can come in from the end with your chisel.

No pin holes are required at this joint because gravity, sheathing, and a large spike or timber screw will hold down the rafters. A ¾-inch pin hole would damage the thin rafter tail excessively at the lap. The old-timers would have used metal fasteners in this situation as well.

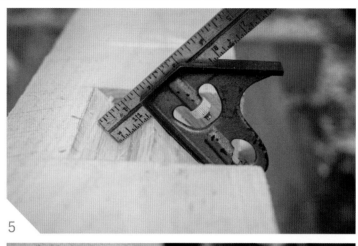

5

THE FINISHED RAFTER SEAT *should provide good bearing, especially in the step. If the entire rafter bears only on the lap, the rafter could split under a load (though it will drop only slightly before coming to bear on the step). If you've cut the step too deep, you could even it out and insert a shim.*

Rafters

Our final pieces to lay out and cut are the rafters. It's a good idea to get out all the rafter timbers and orient them on the horses, placing the *mortised* rafters (east, in our case) on one side and *tenoned* rafters (west) on the other, with the peaks facing each other in the center. This helps you to pick the straightest ones for the ends and put the most-crowned ones together in the middle. Look at the ends of the timbers, and try to put the clearest wood (without knots) down at the tails, where they will be thinned and cantilevered out to form the eaves.

Check the reference faces for square. Reference faces will be the tops of all the rafters and the outside faces of pairs 1, 2, 8, and 9 (counting from the north end). Pairs 3 through 7 will all have the same side as the reference face, and by convention we will pick north. You could just as well pick south as long as you're consistent, since the mortise-and-tenon joint at the peak will be laid out from the layout face on each pair.

THE PEAK JOINT

The 12:12 roof pitch equals a 45-degree slope; this makes cutting the peak joint simple, since the cuts are all square (90 degrees). If you choose a different pitch, the angles will be different (see chapter 7). The step-lap rafter seat will always be cut square to the roof plane, as will the collar mortise. The open mortise-and-tenon at the peak, also called a bridle or *tongue-and-fork* joint, is laid out like all other joints, with the mortise and tenon 1½ inches off the reference face.

The reduced tenoned piece and the mating housing are cut to 4½ inches (the perfect-timber-within). The pin hole is laid out 1½ inches off of each shoulder, and the drawbore on the tenon is made with the drill bit offset slightly toward the tenon shoulder and up toward the top surface, thus drawing the mortised piece in and up against the tenoned piece.

RAFTER LENGTH

The length of the rafters is calculated using the Pythagorean theorem. The rafter forms the hypotenuse of a right triangle, the legs of which are 6 feet each (given our 12:12 roof slope) and represent the run (horizontal span) and rise (vertical height).

RAFTERS

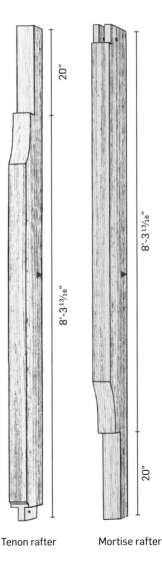

20"

8'-3¹³/₁₆"

8'-3¹³/₁₆"

20"

Tenon rafter   Mortise rafter

RAFTER PEAK DETAIL

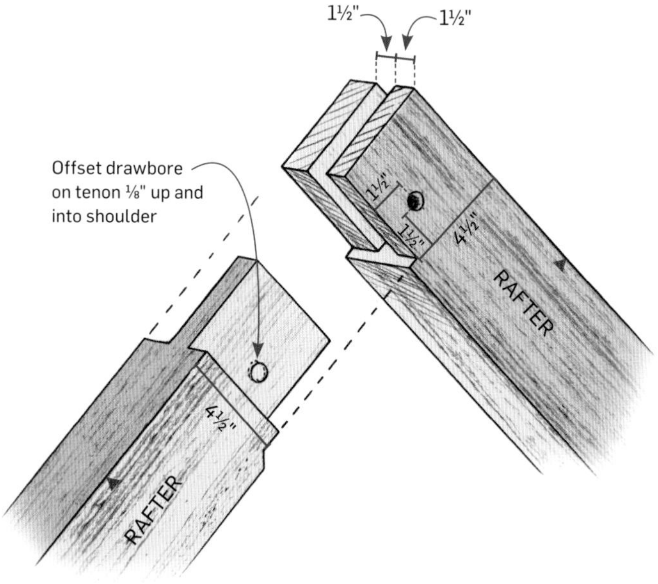

1½"   1½"

Offset drawbore on tenon ⅛" up and into shoulder

1½"

1½"

4½"

RAFTER

4½"

RAFTER

RAFTER TAIL

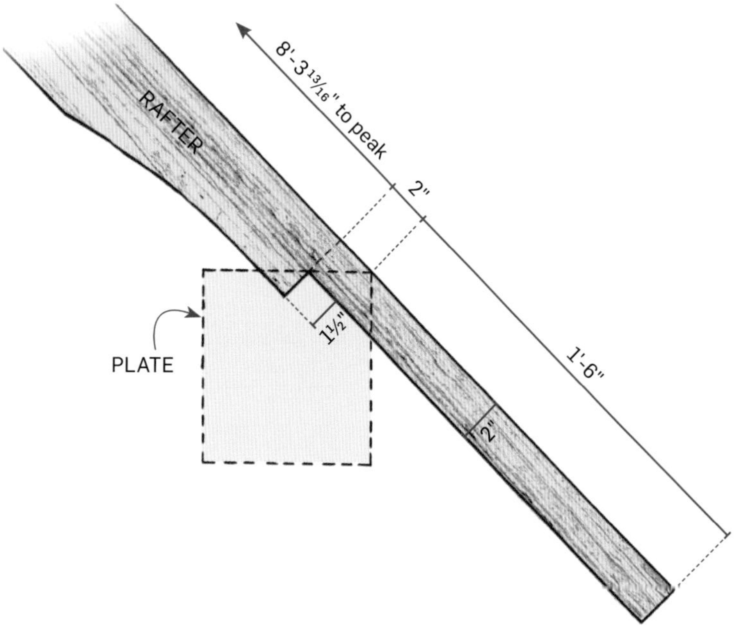

RAFTER

8'-3¹³⁄₁₆" to peak

2"

1½"

PLATE

2"

1'-6"

Calculating the hypotenuse, we get a rafter length of 8 feet 5¹³⁄₁₆ inches from the peak to the outside arris of the plate. Add another 1 foot 6 inches for the tail for a total length of 9 feet 11¹³⁄₁₆ inches. The step for the rafter seat, however, is not cut at the arris of the plate but is up the rafter a bit, and this is the point we want to identify for layout and cutting. Looking at the triangles forming this joint, you can see that this distance is the same as the thickness of the rafter tail, or 2 inches. Thus, the control point we want to mark here is 8 feet 5¹³⁄₁₆ inches down from the peak, minus 2 inches, or 8 feet 3¹³⁄₁₆ inches. The total length of 9 feet 11¹³⁄₁₆ inches remains the same. If you change the pitch of the roof, then all these numbers will also change, and it's best to brush up on geometry and Pythagorus to figure them out.

CUTTING THE SEAT AND TAIL

Cutting the rafter seat and tail involves making a square cross-cut for the seat and then a long rip cut. This rip can be made with a circular saw, bandsaw, or handsaw, but remember that the tail may be visible from underneath, so try not to under-cut it; it's best to leave enough material to clean it up with a hand plane. Since the rafter is 5 inches thick and is reduced down to 3½ inches where it enters the plate, we need to make this transition in the same way we did with the floor joists. This is highly visible on the interior, so a gentle sweeping curve is most pleasing, made with a bandsaw or an axe and adze, followed by a spokeshave.

THE COLLAR MORTISE

The collar mortise and housing (which you will cut on only two pairs of rafters) are cut just like those for a brace. But instead of measuring 30 inches down for one leg of the right triangle of which the brace forms the hypotenuse, measure 5 feet down from the rafter peak and square a line across the rafter to find the "downhill" end of the collar mortise. Then, measure 4½ inches in from the reference (top) surface to establish the housing line, and go back up along this line 7 inches to establish the upper 45-degree end of the collar mortise, just like we did on the brace mortises. Again, if the roof pitch is other than 12:12, the length of the housing and the angles inside will be different, although

the bearing face of the collar is always cut square to the roof plane.

Cut one pair of rafters and check them to verify your layout before cutting the others. Fit the mortise-and-tenon peak together, and measure across from the points on both rafters that represent the outside of the arris of the plate. If it is 12 feet (the width of the building) and the peak looks good, congratulations!

Finally, number the rafter pairs to make sure you have equal numbers of both types and that the reference faces match.

COLLAR MORTISE LAYOUT

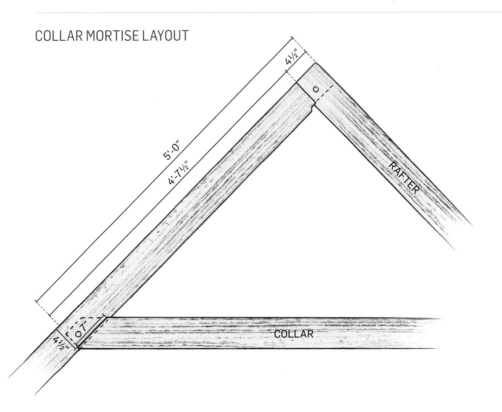

Making Pins

Pins are usually made of a straight-grained hardwood species (oak, hickory, or black locust, for example). They are split out from a green clear log round (*billet*) by quartering it and then riving smaller square "blanks" that are then taken to a shaving horse or jig for final shaping. You can make your own pins, as described below, or you can order them from a supplier (see Resources). Billets can usually be purchased from a logger or sawmill that has the right species; they'll often have a few logs that are longer than they need.

1. LAY OUT THE PINS

Lay out a grid on the end of a 12-inch-long billet. This is long enough for tapered pins going through 7-to-8-inch timbers, and also leaves you some pin sticking out for hanging things on in the finished building. Use a framing square or other gauge to draw two perpendicular lines through the pith of the log (even if off-center) to quarter it. Then draw lines parallel to the first two outward at regular intervals to make a grid of squares; each of these small blanks will yield (theoretically) four pins. The size of these squares should be $\frac{1}{8}$ inch less than twice the diameter of a pin. In other words, to make 1-inch pins, lay out a grid

of $1\frac{7}{8}$-inch squares. Use $1\frac{3}{8}$-inch squares for $\frac{3}{4}$-inch pins. You can rip some strips to these widths on a table saw to act as templates.

2. CUT THE SQUARE BLANKS

Start by placing a froe on a line through the pith, and split the log in half, then split these in half (following the line nearest the pith) to make quarter-logs. Place your froe on the line nearest the center of each remaining piece, and work outward until you have split out the square blanks of the grid. Take these square

2a

2b

1

blanks and quarter them (a smaller froe or an axe helps here) to make the final blanks that will be roughly square. These squares are larger in area than the corresponding round holes, so when the edges are shaved down and tapered to final size, they should still be able to fit snugly.

3. SHAPE THE PINS

Take the square blanks to a shave horse to shape them with a drawknife, or to a bench jig that can be used with a hand plane, slick, or chisel. The jig is a combination bench hook and shooting board with a V-shaped slot in it to hold the pin with one end elevated for tapering. Don't make the pins *too* round; a few ridges left with the drawknife is helpful to key the pin in when it's driven.

Drill holes in the shave horse or work surface to match the diameter of the various pins you'll be making; use the holes as gauges to test-fit the pins.

Start by making the blank square, if it is not square already (often you'll start with a slight parallelogram). Work on the tip end of the pin first, finishing it before turning it around to work on the other end. Place just enough of the back end under the clamp of the shave horse to hold it, and shave square the faces on the rest of the pin. It should take only a few passes, and at the same time you can introduce a slight taper (1/8 inch or so) over the entire length. Then, rotate the blank 45 degrees and take off the edges, with your first pass starting up near the clamp head and the second pass starting about halfway down the pin. When placed in a test hole, the pin should go snug at about the point along its length where the tenon would be. Finally, put a heavy taper on the first couple of inches of the pin to help guide it into the drawbored hole.

3a

3b

CHAPTER 7

VARIATIONS ON THE FRAME

There are a lot of options when it comes to modifying this timber frame, and most involve moving, but not changing, the joinery. The lengths of pieces may also change, but sectional sizes (depth and width of timbers) will remain the same. When more substantial changes are required, we will explain them.

Moving Doors and Windows

Probably the most likely change you'll want to make is the location of doors and windows. The door in the gable end wall has a timber-framed rough opening of 3 feet 6 inches wide by 7 feet 2 inches tall. This is big enough for any prehung exterior door with jambs. On the other hand, you may need to make the opening smaller with some rough-sawn lumber screwed to the timbers to fit the rough opening specified by the door manufacturer. If you acquire the prehung door before cutting the timbers, you can simply locate the door posts wherever they need to be to create the recommended rough opening size.

If you move the door to an eaves wall, note that the plate is much higher than the tie beam, so you may want to frame in a 4×5 timber header since you have the extra room. Dimension the bottom of this header to the rough opening for the door; this will make that face a reference face. You may then have enough room to add a narrow transom window above the door. If you need more room, this member could even be a rough-sawn 2×4 lying flat, since it isn't load bearing.

The door frame may include a threshold; the rough opening specified for such a door will assume that the door unit will be installed on top of a subfloor. Be sure to include the thickness of this subfloor in your layout. Wherever you decide to put your door, remember that the space behind the door is hard to make useful if you want the door to open inward 180 degrees.

One option for utilizing the space behind the door is to frame in a closet, in which case the entry door would open only 90 degrees. Alternatively, you could simply add a coat rack that takes up less space. If you put the door at the end of a wall or bent, the door can open against the adjoining wall. This requires eliminating the brace at the door location, but as long

DOOR AT END OF EAVES WALL

DOORS AND WINDOWS CAN BE MOVED *to anywhere in the frame but may require adding or moving framing members.*

as you have braces resisting racking from both lateral directions elsewhere in the wall, it's not a problem to remove one. Remember that you should have at least one brace that will act in compression depending on the direction of lateral loading in each wall or bent.

The wall girts are meant to be nailers for vertical siding but can also serve as the bottom sills of window rough openings. You can raise or lower them, but the standard height for the bottom of a window is 36 inches from the floor if you want to put a table or couch underneath it, and 42 inches if you want a kitchen sink underneath. From an aesthetic point of view, the tops of doors and windows should be at the same height.

There are no vertical studs shown for windows, to give you more freedom to vary window widths, so you'll need to frame these in. This requires some extra lumber, and since the girts are 4 inches wide, this can easily be done with some rough-sawn 2×4s that you add to your timber order from the sawmill. Planed lumberyard studs won't look as good, nor will they be the right size (too narrow). Your rough-opening members can be cut to exact length and toe-nailed (secured with two nails

DOOR ON EAVE WALL

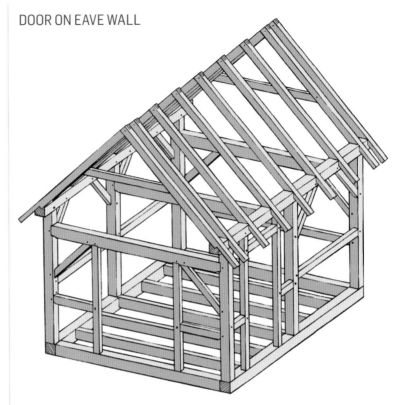

DOORS CAN BE ADDED AND WIDENED *to get large pieces of equipment in, or just to let in more light and air for a studio or workshop.*

LEFT: *Window openings can be framed in with rough-sawn 2×4s.*
RIGHT: *Braces can be moved down to the bottom of the wall if they would interfere with headroom or windows.*

driven at opposite angles) or screwed into the timbers. You can also make some shallow notches to locate them and keep them from twisting, then use toenails to secure them.

You can frame rough-opening members into braces, using beveled end cuts, as long as the brace itself doesn't interfere with the opening. You can also eliminate braces if they're in the way, but it's best to add a replacement elsewhere in the bent or wall to pick up the job in compression. This could be a *down brace* pinned to the sill

and placed directly below an existing upper brace.

Other instances where you may want to move braces are when moving the door to the end of a wall or bent, or if headroom is an issue on an interior brace, such as the braces between the tie beam and center posts in our core frame.

If you lower girts to accommodate windows, you may want to add upper girts in the wall or bent for nailing vertical siding. In the core frame design, the wall plates are higher than the tie beams, and the wall girts

are correspondingly higher than the bent girts. If you are going to use horizontal board siding, you may eliminate the girts entirely and frame in vertical 4×5 studs instead, like the door posts. These should be evenly spaced along the wall every 30 to 36 inches.

Adding a Loft

Adding a loft is an easy way to get more usable space out of these designs, although the headroom will be low, making it mainly appropriate for sleeping. In our core design, the height of an added loft would be a bit less than 7 feet from the loft floor to the peak under the roof. Be aware that a loft cuts down on light coming in from any high windows in the gable end, and for this reason we don't recommend framing an entire second floor at this level. Access is also an issue in such a small space; the best solution our clients have found is some sort of movable ladder: one that slides along like a library ladder, or a hinged ladder you can hoist out of the way. Other ingenious solutions are possible.

If you want more (or less) room in the loft than half the building length, you can move the center bent by a few feet as shown in the accompanying drawing. The 7×8 plate is sized to span up to 10 feet; if you need it to span farther you must increase the size of the plates (see Making the Frame Bigger on page 142).

The joists in the standard-size loft are 4×6, since the span is only 8 feet. The on-center spacing is at 36 to 40 inches, depending on whether you have four or five joists (five joists gives you extra support for heavier loads and also allows you to use thinner flooring). The end joists are framed 12 inches in from the outside of the building. If you increase the span to 10 or 12 feet, the joist size should be increased to 5×6. Alternatively, you could use 4×6s and space them closer together or use a different grade or species, as explained in chapter 2.

The joists are arranged similarly to those in the main floor, with the center joist(s) (two if you have four joists, one if you have five) being a soffit tenon and the others drop-ins, with the pocket laid out 5 inches in from the outside layout face of the north tie beam, and 2 inches into the layout face of the center tie beam. In our core frame, if the loft is framed in the north

LOFT WITH ASYMMETRIC BENTS

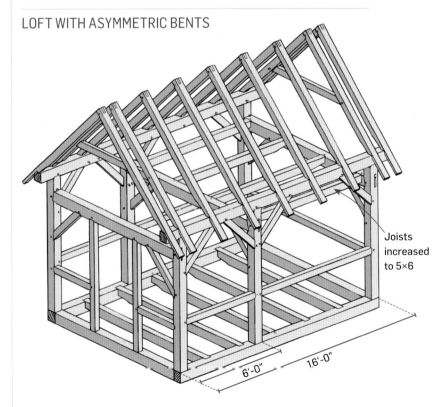

Joists increased to 5×6

6'-0"

16'-0"

LOFT ACCESS *requires some ingenuity, like the folding ladder in upper left, or the removable library ladder in upper right. In the larger 16-foot by 20-foot version of the frame, the partial loft shown at lower left only covers a quarter of the area (8 feet by 10 feet) and is used mostly for storage. Even in the smaller 10-foot-wide version of the frame, the loft (lower right) can still be an attractive and useable space.*

bay, the shoulder-to-shoulder length of the soffit-tenoned joists is 7 feet 8½ inches minus 6½ inches plus ½ inch, or 7 feet 2½ inches (just like the girts). Add 4-inch nominal (3⅞ inches actual) tenons. The drop-in joists have an end-to-end length of 7 feet 8½ inches minus 5 inches plus 2 inches, or 7 feet 5½ inches; then subtract an extra ¼ inch overall for clearance at the back of the pockets.

Reduce the joists down to 4½ inches in height where they enter the tie beams, just like with the lower joists.

If you want more headroom in the loft, you have a few options. You could make the building wider (see Making the Frame Bigger on page 142) or increase the roof pitch; both changes make the rafters longer. You could also make the posts longer, but the distance from the top of the tie beam to top of the plate should not exceed 2 feet with 7×7 posts. If you want to go higher (up to 4 feet between the tops of the plate and beam),

you should increase the post size to 8×8. This means most of your other timbers also need to be increased in size so that widths match. Going to 7×9 posts is another option, with the depth of the post increased to resist the greater force on the top of the post. As the post gets longer, the plate (which is carrying the outward thrust of the rafters) gets further away from the restraint of the tie beam. This means that the post has to be thicker to resist the bending imposed by the roof.

LOFT JOISTS FOR CORE FRAME

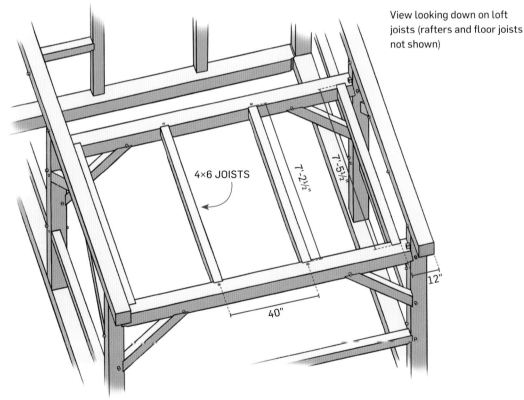

View looking down on loft joists (rafters and floor joists not shown)

4×6 JOISTS

7'-2½"

7'-5½"

40"

12"

Changing the Roof Pitch

The 12:12 roof pitch on our core frame is relatively easy to lay out and cut because all of the angles are 45 or 90 degrees. Once you change that pitch the peak and seat joints become a bit trickier.

You may want to lower the pitch for aesthetic reasons, such as to match an existing building on-site, but you'll lose headroom in the loft (should you want one). As the roof gets flatter, the outward thrust on the plates also increases. To resist this horizontal bending on lower-pitched roofs, we turn the plate on its side so it becomes an 8×7 instead of a 7×8. Since the plate is now wider than the 7-inch posts, you can map the housings to match the tops of the posts, or just let the housing go all the way across and accept the visual consequences (it's much easier to cut).

The bridle joint at the peak will have angles other than 90 degrees if the roof pitch changes from 12:12, and it would be useful to make a template for laying out the mortise and tenon. On the view below, note how we extended the reductions on both the mortised and tenoned rafters. This makes it easier to cut than an acute shoulder, and it looks better.

8:12 ROOF PITCH

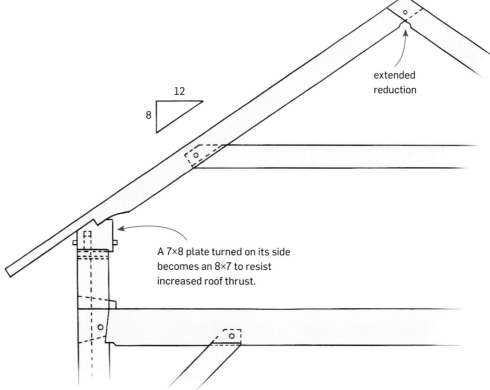

extended reduction

12

8

A 7×8 plate turned on its side becomes an 8×7 to resist increased roof thrust.

The step-lap rafter seat also changes as the roof pitch changes. As the roof gets shallower, the lines for the back of the joint on the top of the plate move inward, and the line on the face of the plate moves up; the opposite happens as the pitch gets steeper. You can calculate these shifts by using the Pythagorean theorem, or create a drawing with your framing square to help you see it, and take the measurements right off the drawing. The illustration below shows the adjusted measurements for a step-lap rafter seat for an 8:12 roof.

MAKING A ROOF PEAK TEMPLATE

Use the following instructions to create a template for an 8:12 roof pitch. You can make templates for other pitches by holding the appropriate *rise* on the tongue of a framing square, and the *run* on the blade.

1 Start with a piece of ¼-inch plywood about 24 inches by 16 inches square, with one good 24-inch edge. From one corner of this straight edge, measure 6 inches over along the edge and make a mark.

2 With a framing square, hold 8 inches on the tongue (the narrower arm) on this mark and rotate the square until 12 inches on the blade (the wider arm) is aligned farther down the straight edge. Draw a line (shown on the facing page as Line 1) down the tongue from the mark to represent a plumb line, and extend this line all the way across the plywood.

3 Keeping the 8-inch point on the mark, rotate the square until the 12-inch point on the blade intersects the plumb line. Draw another line (Line 2) as long as possible from your original mark along the tongue; this represents the opposite roof pitch and the end of the rafter. The straight edge represents the top (outside face) of the rafter, and the 6-inch mark you made is the peak.

4 Measure 5 inches down from your straight edge, and draw a parallel line (Line 3) across the board (5 inches is the nominal thickness of the rafters in our frame). Draw another line (Line 4) 5 inches from and parallel to Line 2. Don't extend these lines past where they intersect. They represent the bottoms of the rafters.

STEP-LAP ADJUSTED FOR 8:12 ROOF PITCH

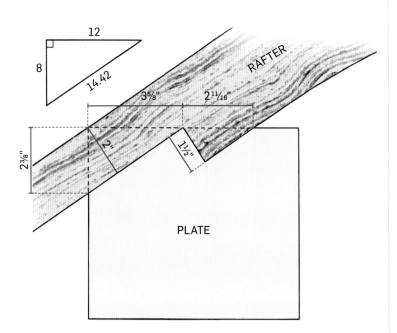

5 Since the rafters get reduced to 4½ inches at the peak, draw another set of parallel lines at that distance. One of these lines can be solid to represent the mortised piece and the other dashed to represent the tenon.

6 We will reduce both rafters 1½ inches back from the shoulder, using a bevel cut parallel to the plumb line. This allows us to use the template for both mortised and tenoned rafters, and it avoids an acute angle on the shoulder and also looks better. Once you have it all laid out, you can carefully cut out the template and use it for both sides of the rafter joint, making a small notch in the template to represent the shoulder of the joint. Register the top edge and peak of the template to your rafters to mark the joint.

ROOF PEAK TEMPLATE: STEPS 1, 2, AND 3

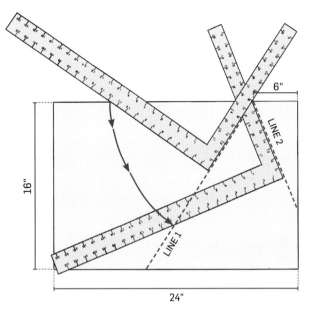

ROOF PEAK TEMPLATE: STEPS 4, 5, AND 6

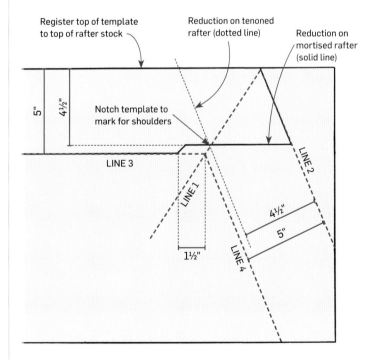

Overhangs

The rafter tails in our core project extend 16 inches past the plate to form the eaves, and the plates extend 12 inches beyond the gable ends to create an overhang. You may want more overhang, depending on how thick your enclosure system is and how much you want to protect it. For 2-inch-thick rafter tails, 18 inches is close to the limit; if you want more (up to 30 inches) you should increase the rafter tail thickness to 3 inches. This will result in the rafters sticking up 1 inch above the arris of the plate, but you can close that off with beveled strips between the rafters before you sheath the roof. It's possible to extend the rafter tails out to 48 inches (maybe for firewood storage), but in this case you should support the overhang with a braced 2×4 "outrigger" and increase the tail thickness to 3½ inches.

The plates could extend out to 24 inches without being increased in size, and even further if you add external braces. This would allow you to have a small porch or covered entry. If you are using the frame as an addition to an existing building you can eliminate the gable overhang on the end that joins the other structure.

THE RAFTER PLATES CAN BE EXTENDED ON THE EXTERIOR *to form a porch or door overhang.*

LONGER RAFTER TAILS (UP TO 30 INCHES)

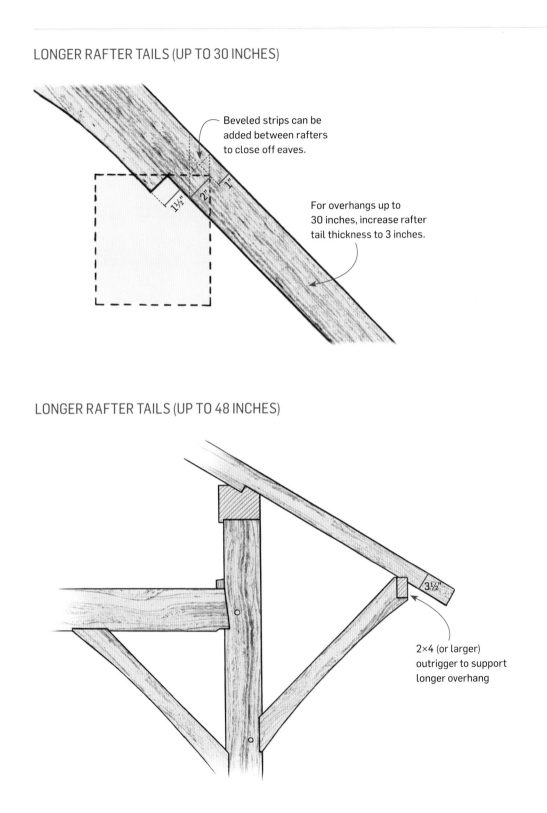

Beveled strips can be added between rafters to close off eaves.

1½"

2"

1"

For overhangs up to 30 inches, increase rafter tail thickness to 3 inches.

LONGER RAFTER TAILS (UP TO 48 INCHES)

3½"

2×4 (or larger) outrigger to support longer overhang

Making the Frame Smaller

Making the frame smaller will not affect the sectional dimensions of pieces, since the joinery still requires a minimum amount of wood to be functional. Lengths will change, and if you reduce the building to less than 12 feet in length, you can eliminate the center bent. If the plate span increases to over 10 feet, however, you should increase the size of the plate to 7×9 and get a No. 1 grade timber.

THIS MEDITATION CABIN *is 10 feet wide by 14 feet 6 inches long and includes a half-loft and covered entry.*

10'×14'-6" FRAME WITH LONGER PLATE OVERHANG

This is the frame for
the structure at left.

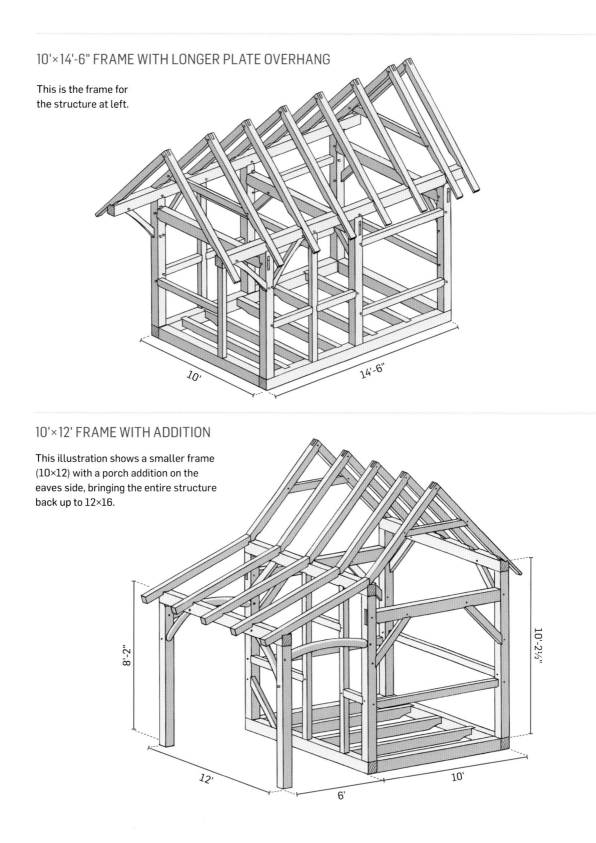

10'×12' FRAME WITH ADDITION

This illustration shows a smaller frame
(10×12) with a porch addition on the
eaves side, bringing the entire structure
back up to 12×16.

Making the Frame Bigger

Increasing the three-bent frame up to 14 feet in width and 20 feet in length won't increase the size of the timbers, except for main-floor joists, which should be increased to 5×8 or go up to No. 1 grade. When the building increases to 16 feet in width, add a central 10×8 girder to the floor frame and a central foundation pier. In this case, the joists would drop into pockets on both sides of the girder, so the extra width is required. Again, if the plate span increases to over 10 feet, you should increase it to a 7×9 and get a No. 1 grade timber. If the tie beams are going to carry a loft, increase their size to 7×9.

Instead of using 7×9 plates and tie beams, you could increase the posts — and the major timbers joining to them — to 8 inches in width. A No. 1 grade 8×8 plate can span up to 12 feet on a frame 16 feet wide (use an 8×10 timber if No. 2 grade). If you can't get plate timbers long enough to span the entire building length (including overhangs), it's possible to scarf the timbers together, making an end-to-end joint to make one long timber out of two shorter ones. This is more work,

FLOOR FRAME FOR A 16' × 20' STRUCTURE

If the foundation is not continuous, piers should be placed under each post and in the center of cross sills as shown.

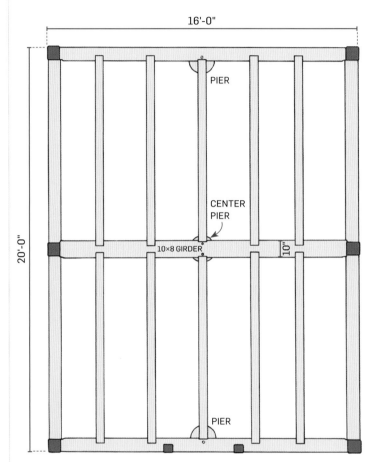

Structural Support

If these structural options are confusing, it's a good idea to learn the basic engineering calculations for sizing beams, or get a spreadsheet that has the formulas built in. There are many combinations of size, grade, species, and spacing that can be found to work in any given situation. Your best option, of course, is to get your design reviewed by a qualified professional.

however, and not as strong as a single full-length timber.

The 5×5 rafters will work up to a 16-foot-wide roof span, given the design's snow load and roof pitch.

One of the best ways to expand the basic 12×16 frame is simply to add modules to it. Multiple 8×12 sections can be added to the gable ends to make a building as long as you want, with scarf joints used to extend the plates and sills, if you can't get timbers long enough.

Adding an extension to the eaves walls requires extending the roof rafters. If you maintain the same pitch as the main roof, the outer extension wall will have to be shorter to carry the rafters.

As you can see, a lower pitch, such as 8:12, makes it easier to extend the roof, rather than having to change the slope partway down. Alternatively, you can change the extension roof to a shallower pitch and/or make the main posts taller. Examples are shown on pages 148–149.

Note that tie beams are required to connect the extended wall to the core frame, and these come in to the center posts slightly lower than the main ties. The lower ties connect to the outer plate on the addition at the same elevation to conserve

SCARF JOINTS

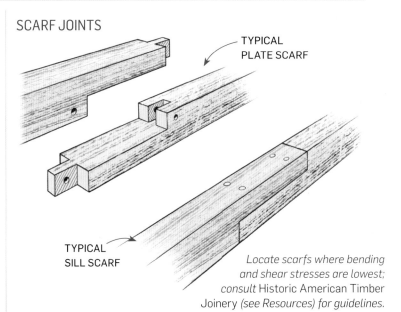

TYPICAL PLATE SCARF

TYPICAL SILL SCARF

Locate scarfs where bending and shear stresses are lowest; consult Historic American Timber Joinery *(see Resources) for guidelines.*

A 4-FOOT EXTENSION ON THE REAR EAVES WALL *of this frame is made possible by the lower-pitched roof.*

EAVES WALL EXTENSION

This version uses an off-center middle bent to create a larger bay for the tractor. Note that the rear tie beam meets the post at a lower point than the main tie beam and therefore needs just a simple mortise-and-tenon joint. However, on the rear wall, they join the plate at the same height, and thus need the joinery shown on page 146.

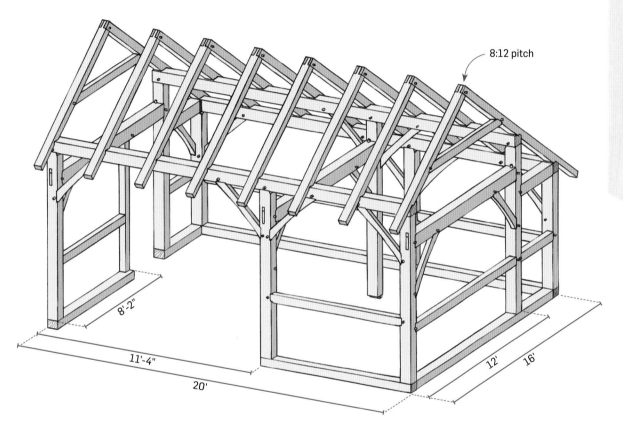

8:12 pitch

8'-2"

11'-4"

20'

12'   16'

height. Because the outer posts are coming into the same plate from below, this condition requires different joinery, as shown in the detail below.

The rafters are supported on both ends, so there is no thrust on the joint between the tie beam and plate. This contributes to the joint's simplicity, since it doesn't need to provide tying action. This lack of thrust on the rafter foot allows us to use a simpler *birdsmouth* joint, as shown, instead of a step lap.

THE SPLINE JOINT

In the frame shown on the previous page, the extension tie beams come in low enough not to interfere with the wedged dovetail tying joint of the main ties. In this case, these outer ties can have a simple 4-inch tenon at each end. If the tie beams are close enough to interfere with each other, a spline joint can be used to connect them together and provide the tying action required.

A spline is a separate piece of hardwood or LVL (laminated veneer lumber) that is used to join beams coming into opposite sides of a post at the same (or nearly the same) elevation. Because there is not enough room within the post for sufficiently long tenons on the end of each beam, the spline passes through the post, extends into a long mortise in each beam, and then is pinned to each. Thus, one beam is directly attached to the other, with no pins needed in the post. This is especially helpful if the joint must have some tying capacity.

BEAM AND PLATE MEETING AT TOP OF POST

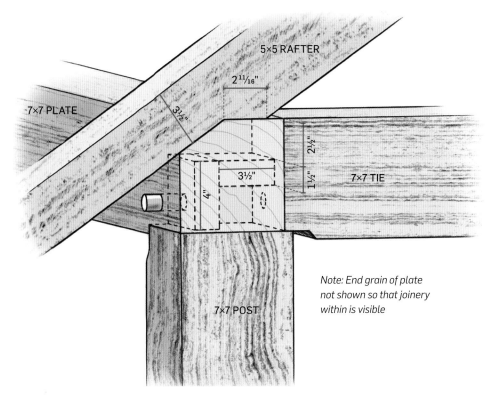

5×5 RAFTER

2¹¹⁄₁₆"

7×7 PLATE

3½"

2½"

3½"

1½"

4"

7×7 TIE

7×7 POST

Note: End grain of plate not shown so that joinery within is visible

Splines should be long enough to extend at least 14 inches into each beam (16 inches is better), and are 1½ inches thick (or 1¾ inches thick if you are using LVL) by 3½ inches wide (5½ inches for beams over 10 inches deep). Two pins are sufficient in each end of the spline, about 4 inches apart and slightly staggered so they aren't in line along the grain. This is not an issue in an LVL, but in solid wood the fibers are arranged longitudinally, and the tension stress in the spline could cause the wood to split if concentrated along one shear plane. By staggering the pins the stress is distributed along multiple planes of fiber. The outer pins should be about 5 inches from the ends of the spline. If the beams are at slightly different heights, the spline can go into the top part of the lower beam and the bottom of the upper beam.

You don't see many splines in older timber frames because the long mortises were difficult to make — and still are with hand tools. Today, power saws and chain mortisers make this difficult joint easier to execute, helping to solve this tricky problem of beams meeting at the same height on a post.

SPLINE JOINT

A hardwood spline is 1½" wide × 3½" deep, laid out 2½" from layout face.

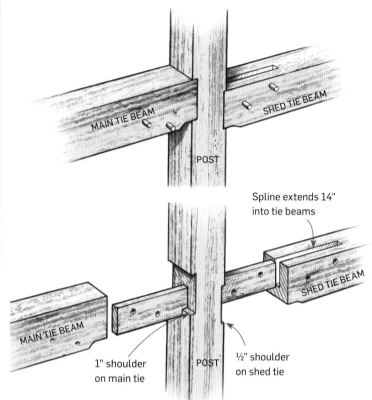

THIS "OVER-AND-UNDER" SPLINE *goes into the top of one beam and the bottom of the other. Splines are often used to connect beams coming into all four faces of a post at the same elevation.*

ADDING AN 8' × 8' ADDITION

An 8-foot-wide addition on the eaves wall will require a change in the roof pitch. Since the tie beams for the addition are close to the main tie beams in elevation, they require spline joinery as shown on page 147.

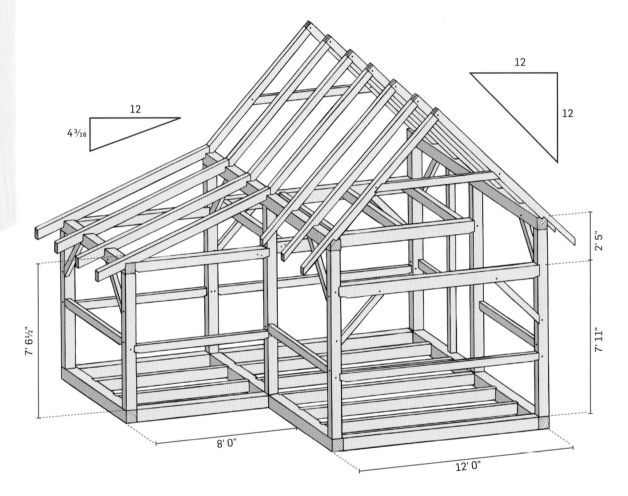

ADDING A 10' × 16' ADDITION

This full 10-foot addition to the eaves wall requires an even lower-pitched roof (3⁵⁄₁₆:12), and the main roof is lowered to 10:12. In cold climates, the intersection of the two roofs should be sealed well with an ice and water shield.

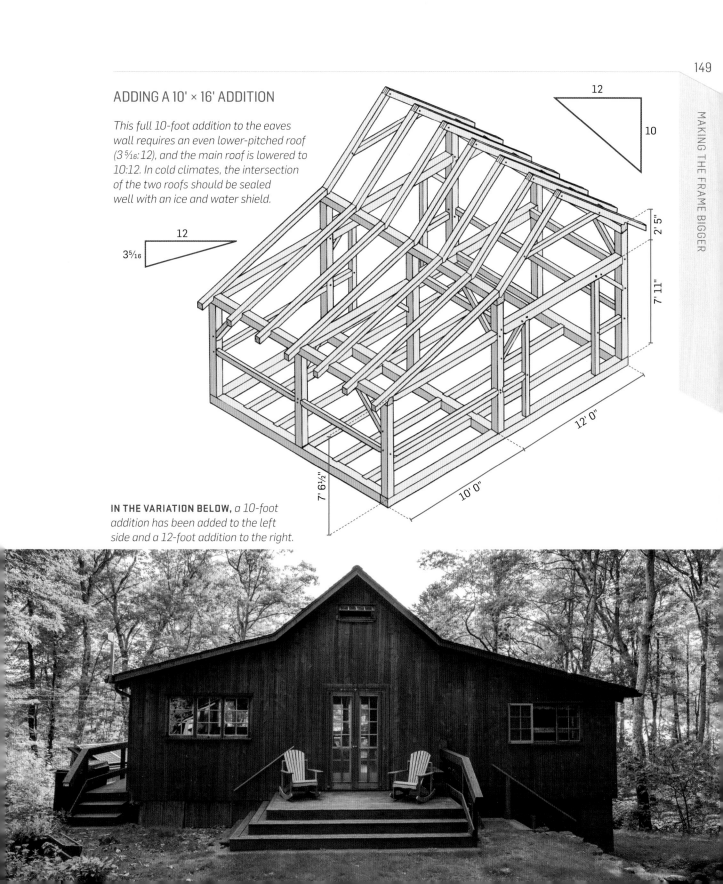

IN THE VARIATION BELOW, *a 10-foot addition has been added to the left side and a 12-foot addition to the right.*

CHAPTER 8

RAISING THE FRAME

Once your joinery is complete, you finally get the reward for all your hard work: raising day! There is a tremendous amount of satisfaction in seeing your frame come together, but with it comes a responsibility to erect it safely and efficiently.

Equipment for Raising Day

There are a number of methods and equipment to help with the raising, such as cranes and gin poles, which we would use on larger frames or if we had only a few people to assist. The core frame described here can be raised easily by a dozen or so friends, as long as you provide adequate support for people to stand on. This would include at least 12 high-quality planks (2×8s or 2×10s) that are long enough to span the length of the structure. These planks can go down on the floor frame after it is assembled so you can put the bents together. After the bents are up and braced, with the wall girts installed, the planks can be moved up onto the tie beams for people to stand on while the plates are handed up. Four planks should go along each outer wall and another four down the center for pegging the rafter peaks.

Twelve cutoff timber ends of equal size (don't discard these as you are working on your timbers!) should be used to block up the bents prior to raising so that people can get their hands underneath. You will also want to have at least four 10-foot-long 2×4s on hand for temporarily bracing the bents, and heavy duty timber screws or duplex nails to secure them.

Additional equipment to have on hand includes a ladder and at least one pair of sawhorses. You may find it easiest to lift a bent partway and support it on the horses while you regroup for the final lift. Optional gear might include ropes and come-alongs or ratchet straps for pulling the bents together, although with proper joinery and drawboring we usually find these unnecessary. If you have to force your joinery together, it's too tight.

WHEN PREPARING YOUR SITE, *remove as many obstacles as possible and smooth the area around the foundation. This will make carrying heavy timber and tools safer and easier. It's better to hand a timber over to someone on the other side of an obstacle rather than try to carry it while you step over.*

Reminders

First, a few important things to keep in mind throughout the raising process:

→ Before assembling any mortise-and-tenon joints, be sure that the mortises are clear of chips and other debris. It's also a good idea to confirm that tenons are not oversized and mortises are deep enough. It's easy to forget to add the housing depth when boring a mortise.

→ Pins should be tapered to pull the drawbore up tight.

→ Before driving any pins, look into the pin hole to make sure it's clear and the drawbore is not too great (you should be able to see at least half of the pin hole in the tenon).

→ Drive all pins from the layout face, and hit them squarely to avoid splitting them.

BE SAFE!

The Occupational Health and Safety Administration (OSHA) mandates fall prevention and other procedures for paid employees but doesn't for unpaid volunteers. Nevertheless, as the owner of the property and organizer of the raising event, you are responsible for providing as safe a working environment as reasonably possible for your raising crew, given the size of the building and the duration of the event.

→ Ladders should be of adequate length and well secured at top and bottom.

→ Your family and friends should be physically fit enough to climb on the frame and lift heavy objects.

→ Have a safety meeting before the raising to identify hazards and inform everyone of the sequence of events.

→ Designate a responsible person who won't be up on the frame to monitor the site and proceedings and identify and communicate hazards to the rest of the crew as they occur.

→ Require hard hats for anyone working beneath timbers or other people.

→ Never leave a tool lying on a timber where it could fall and hit someone below.

→ Take as few tools as necessary aloft during roof framing; all must be well-secured to their users.

→ Planks for standing on should not have saw cuts or large knots and be at least 1½ inches thick. Doubling them up to make the platform 3 inches thick and covering the whole area on top of the tie beams is even safer. If you already have boards for your wall and roof sheathing, you can use these, provided they're thick enough.

→ Stop all other work when a chisel is being used.

→ Listen carefully to the raising leader, keep unnecessary chatter to a minimum, and always be aware of what's going on around you.

The Raising Script

Before raising, it's good to write a script to help you envision every step in the process and anticipate any problems that might occur. The following instructions comprise a sample script for raising the 12×16 core frame.

ASSEMBLING THE FLOOR FRAME

1 Place one of the long sills on the foundation. Insert the tenons of the two short sills and soffit-tenoned joists, and *lightly* snug up the joints with pins to hold the joints together while working on the opposite long sill. Fit the other long sill into place. Confirm that all joints will go together (no thick or wide tenons, nor too-small mortises), then drive the pins just enough to snug up all the shoulders on the joints.

2 Measure the diagonals — from corner to opposite corner — to roughly square up the frame on the foundation; the diagonal measurements should be close to equal. *Then* drive home the pins, making sure to stop driving when the pins hit the foundation underneath (see Pin Tips, page 154).

1

2

Pin Tips

→ **Don't drive pins home** in any assembly until you are sure all pieces will fit and the dimensions are correct. It is not uncommon to find a mistake, such as a misaligned pin hole or mortise in the wrong location, that may require taking the assembly apart to work on a piece. If one part of the assembly has already been pinned tightly, it may be hard to remove the pins.

→ **Cut off pins** flush with the floor after they are fully secured. On other assemblies, such as the walls and roof, cut off pins on the outside, where they will be covered by sheathing. On the inside they can be left long to be used as hooks, unless they are at eye level or pose some other hazard.

3 Shim the floor frame (if necessary) until it is level. Do the final squaring up of the floor frame by measuring the diagonals and adjusting the frame until they are exactly equal (within ¼ inch). Drop in remaining joists. Lay temporary planking or plywood over the floor frame for safety.

ASSEMBLING AND RAISING THE BENTS

1 Assemble Bent 1 on the floor frame with the stub tenons on the bottoms of the posts lined up over the mortises. All bents are assembled with the reference faces up. Work the posts onto the wedged dovetail tenons on the tie beam while inserting the braces and girts. Snug up the joints with pins, alternately driving the wedge and the 1-inch pin on the dovetail joint. When all joints appear to fit well, drive the pins home, always being aware of what the pin could hit underneath.

3

1

2 Raise Bent 1. Position two people on the foot of each post to make sure the stub tenons start into their mortises cleanly. Use the commander to adjust as needed. Make sure that people keep their hands out from under the post bottoms; a pry bar can be useful to adjust and hold up the post as you locate it into the sill mortise. Secure the bent plumb with temporary bracing (2b).

2a

TIMBER TIP

Before raising the first bent, drop a coin with the current year's date into a stub tenon mortise (tradition!).

2b

3

 Assemble and raise Bents 2 and 3 following the same procedure as Bent 1. Insert bay girts as necessary while raising.

4 Place planking across the tie beams (or erect staging) to stand on.

4

RAISING THE PLATES

1 Use ropes to lift the plates up to that level (parbuckling) or hand them up if you have enough people.

2 Insert the plate braces into the posts, and hold them in place with snugged-up pins in the posts. Lift the plates onto the tenons in the posts and braces, with people on each brace to make sure it feeds into its mortise (2a). Use the commander to adjust, as necessary (2b).

1

2a

2b

Parbuckling

What do the ill-fated cruise ship *Costa Concordia* and timber framing have in common? The capsized vessel (along with many other sunken ships throughout history) was raised upright with parbuckling, a traditional method of raising cylindrical objects using rotational leverage. Loggers have often used it to roll logs up and onto trucks for transport.

The process involves running ropes down from the top of the posts (tie them through the pin holes), under the plate resting on sawhorses below, and back up the outside of the plate to people above. Keep the ropes out of the joinery locations if possible. The personnel up top now have a 2:1 mechanical advantage and can easily roll the timber up the side of the frame as they pull the ropes. People below may have to guide the timber around pins or wedges if they haven't been cut off.

When the timber reaches the top, the crew will have to lift it over the post tenons and rest it there or on the planking while they remove the ropes from the pin holes, then install it. In a perfect world, the plate, as it's lifted, would rotate just the exact number of times for the mortises to flip right onto the tenons — but that would make removing the ropes tough!

RAISING THE RAFTERS

1 Place planks across the tie beams in the center of the building, or across the plates between rafter seats at one end of the frame, in order to reach the rafter peaks. Assemble the first pair of rafters with the collar tie on the ground, and lift the assembly up to the roof crew, being careful not to stress the rafter tails (1a). If there is an end pair without collars on the gable overhang, set the assembled pair with the collar on the planking behind the installation crew and hand up the two end rafters individually. Install this end pair first, before setting the assembled pair with collars.

Secure the rafter tails to the rafter seats with two 20d toenails or 4-inch timber screws, making sure the rafters are plumb (1b). Although the rafters could be held there by gravity without being secured, any uplift on the rafter tails (or suction on the roof caused by wind going over it) could lift the rafters. Screws act like clamps, and thus hold the roof down better than any wooden pin, which would take out more wood from the rafter than a nail or screw.

1a

1b

The easiest way to check for plumb is to use a long level or plumb bob to make sure the faces of the rafters (those that are flush to the outside of the lower frame) are plumb over the tie beam's outside face.

Slide planks along the plates as other rafters are handed up individually and pinned at the peak. No need to plumb these rafters yet as you'll do so in the next step by spacing them after all are in place.

2 Assemble the last rafter pair on the ground with the collar tie, and hand it up to the roof crew to install (2a). Plumb the end rafters over the tie beam (2b), and nail spacer boards diagonally across all rafters to maintain proper spacing. These can be the 2×4s you used earlier for bracing the bents, screwed into the underside of the rafters. These will stay on until your roof sheathing is installed, holding the rafters in place.

3 Top off the frame by nailing up the wetting bush, and celebrate a job well done!

2a

2b

3

*The **wetting bush** is the ceremonial tree branch (of the same species as the frame, ideally) that is nailed to the peak once the roof frame is complete. This symbolically re-establishes the roots of the building for longevity and expresses gratitude to the trees that create the structure.*

Removing Pins

If you need to remove pins, there are several methods to try:

→ **Punch-bolt (A):** Find a long (10 inches or so) ½-inch diameter bolt, and drill a slight concave depression in the end opposite the bolt head. This depression can then locate on the pin point to drive the pin back out from the side opposite the way it went in.

→ **Dent puller:** If you can find a dent puller (with a sliding handle) that can accept a ⅛-inch screw in the end, screw that into the end grain of the pin and pull it out like you're removing a dent in sheet metal.

→ **Timber screw (B):** Screw a timber screw into the end grain of the pin and use a wrecking bar to pry out the pin. This doesn't always work, as the screw tends to split the pin.

→ **Claw hammer (C):** The most common causes of a pin that is stuck or needs pulling are when there is too much drawbore or the pin starts to break when it's only partway in. Take a straight-claw hammer, and set the claw into the pin right at the timber surface. Repeatedly strike the hammer head with a mallet, lifting the claw as if you're pulling a nail. Reset the claw as the pin backs out.

Warning: Wear safety glasses! Hitting the hardened-steel head of a hammer with another hardened-steel tool can cause either tool to shatter and send out shrapnel.

A

B

C

CHAPTER 9

FOUNDATIONS & ENCLOSURE SYSTEMS

The timber frame is just one component of the building *system*, and you must consider how it will work with the other components. Here we'll explain the basic options for foundations, enclosure, and insulation; these are the components most affected by the type of framing system used and vice-versa. The rest of your finishing options, such as flooring, trim, doors, and windows, will be the same regardless of the framing system.

Foundations

These frames should be placed on a continuous foundation or on piers placed under each post location. Many building departments won't require an extensive foundation that extends below the frost line for auxiliary buildings such as storage sheds. If there is no plumbing, then the building could "float" on pads, stones, or blocks placed in a shallow bed of crushed stone (at least ¾-inch diameter). Such a foundation would be appropriate if you want to move the structure someday (they are certainly small enough) or attach it to a larger structure later.

It's helpful to understand the nature of frost action if considering such a floating foundation, since frost can lift with great pressure anything it gets underneath. If the site is well drained, then water won't collect in the crushed-stone bed; the air spaces between the crushed stone will also give any frost room to expand without heaving. Mound up the stone at each pad and make sure that the ground slopes away on all sides.

If you are going to insulate the floor between the joists, you may want to raise it up on the foundation at least 18 inches so you can get underneath later if need be. This will also help keep critters and moisture from getting into the system, and you can insulate and enclose the underside later after the roof is on.

CONCRETE FOUNDATIONS

If the frame is going to be attached to a larger building, or you just want to have a "rock-solid" foundation that can't move, then you will want to go below frost line (if you have one) with piers or a continuous wall and footing to get the frame well up off the ground. While piers are simple to build, they leave the area under the structure open to the environment. A continuous wall would enclose this crawl space and keep it warmer. Piers or continuous walls can be built from rot-resistant wood (such as white oak or locust, or wood with foundation-grade pressure treatment) or concrete block, but in our area most are built with concrete poured into a form.

THESE 8-INCH-DIAMETER CONCRETE PIERS *are inset from the outside dimensions of the frame so that the siding can extend down past the top of the pier.*

FOUNDATION PLAN

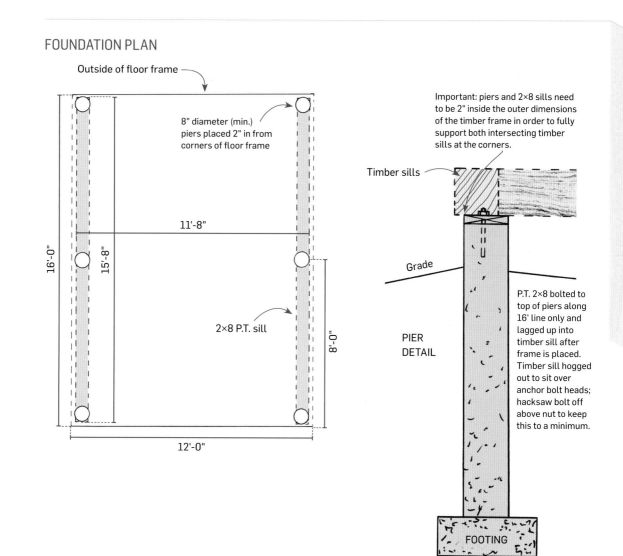

Outside of floor frame

8" diameter (min.) piers placed 2" in from corners of floor frame

11'-8"

16'-0"

15'-8"

2×8 P.T. sill

8'-0"

12'-0"

Important: piers and 2×8 sills need to be 2" inside the outer dimensions of the timber frame in order to fully support both intersecting timber sills at the corners.

Timber sills

Grade

PIER DETAIL

P.T. 2×8 bolted to top of piers along 16' line only and lagged up into timber sill after frame is placed. Timber sill hogged out to sit over anchor bolt heads; hacksaw bolt off above nut to keep this to a minimum.

FOOTING

An example of a pier foundation with footings that extend below the frost line is shown in the Foundation Plan drawing. If you are using poured concrete piers with anchor bolts, it's best to place the piers so that no part of them extends beyond the building edge, where they could create a shelf that would collect water. To be sure, bring the piers 2 inches in from the outside dimensions (see drawing); this also provides additional support for the joints connecting the sills. Bolt pressure-treated (P.T.) 2×8s across the tops of piers to tie them together. After the frame is raised, drive timber screws up through this lumber and into the bottoms of the timber sills. These 2×8s should not extend outside of the timber sills; the wall sheathing can run down past them and be nailed to them for extra stability.

A frame can also go on any type of continuous foundation, such as a poured concrete wall or slab. In this case, there is no need for a timber-framed floor system, since the sills do not need to span open space. A rot-resistant 2×6 is usually bolted down and a conventional stick-framed floor built on top of that (if it is not a slab foundation). The posts should rest on built-up blocking in the floor joists below, and the stub tenons should go into mortises you create in the subfloor. Place the blocking so that its grain is vertical to minimize the effects of shrinkage. The exterior wall sheathing should overhang and be nailed into this sill if possible, to hold the structure down.

Details for the frame-to-foundation connection will also depend on how you are going to insulate the structure, if at all.

FRAME TO FOUNDATION DETAIL

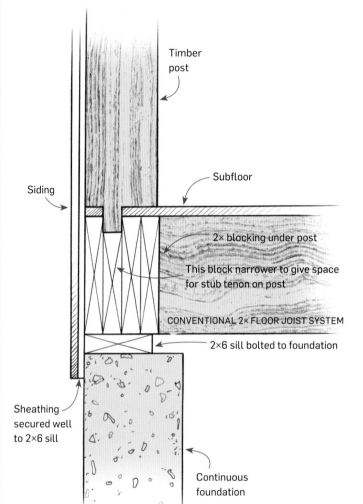

Timber post

Subfloor

Siding

2× blocking under post

This block narrower to give space for stub tenon on post

CONVENTIONAL 2× FLOOR JOIST SYSTEM

2×6 sill bolted to foundation

Sheathing secured well to 2×6 sill

Continuous foundation

Insulation and Enclosure

A tiny timber frame like these can be heated very rapidly with a small gas, wood, or electric heater. For occasional heating you may not need much insulation, but for full-time winter use in cold climates, you'll want more than just the boards, siding, and roofing you might use on a storage shed.

Although you may be tempted to expose the timber frame on the outside as well as the inside, like a traditional infilled frame in Europe, don't consider doing this in a cold climate in North America. In cold climates it's important to completely enclose the timber frame in an insulated envelope. Without this separate thermal barrier, timbers can shrink and open up gaps in an infill system, leading to condensation and rot.

WRAP AND STRAP

One insulation and enclosure system is known as "wrap and strap" and involves building up layers from the inside out. A typical profile might include a drywall or wooden tongue-and-groove interior, 1½ inches or more of extruded polystyrene or polyisocyanurate foam insulation with vertical or horizontal 2×4 strapping, housewrap air barrier, and then horizontal or vertical siding nailed to strapping.

An identical system could be used on the roof, although you may want to eliminate the rafter tails for better air-sealing. In that case, add a second layer of strapping to cantilever out and form the eaves and also provide venting for the roof. The direction of the strapping, and whether to use plywood sheathing, will depend on the type of roofing you choose.

The 2×4 strapping in the walls and roof must run perpendicular to timbers. In the walls, it can run vertically across the girts or horizontally across the posts; it will run horizontally across the rafters. The strapping is secured with timber screws driven through the interior finish and at least 1½ inches into the timbers. If you add a second layer of insulation and strapping, it should run perpendicular to the first. You can even use vertical studs in the timber frame rather than horizontal girts, if it makes the rest of the system easier (for example, if you want horizontal boards on the interior).

At the bottom of the wall system, screw a continuous strip — 1½ inches thick — to close it off to invaders like mice and ants. If you are going for a thicker wall system, it's best to use a wider bottom sill below the floor and use it to support the wall insulation system as well as to insulate the edge of the floor framing. For wood siding, it is also advisable to have a ¾-inch air space or a rain screen behind the siding to aid in drying; screening at the bottom can provide airflow while keeping out pests.

If you are adding more than just a layer or two of boards to the outside of your frame, the doors and windows will typically be supported by the same framing that carries the insulation, rather than by the timber frame.

All of these options for the walls will affect the installation and trimming of doors and windows. Consulting a good building book (see Resources) or a qualified building professional is a good idea when working out the details.

The following illustrations show four wrap-and-strap options, with horizontal or vertical siding and varying levels of insulation.

Wrap and Strap: Four Options

A. R-10 INSULATION, HORIZONTAL SIDING

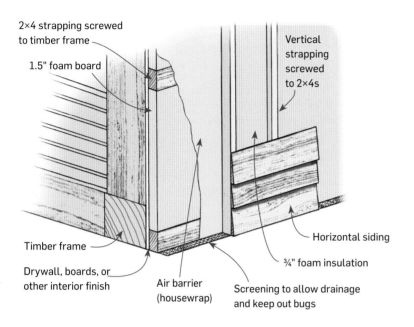

2×4 strapping screwed to timber frame

1.5" foam board

Vertical strapping screwed to 2×4s

Timber frame

Drywall, boards, or other interior finish

Air barrier (housewrap)

¾" foam insulation

Horizontal siding

Screening to allow drainage and keep out bugs

B. R-7.5 INSULATION, HORIZONTAL SIDING

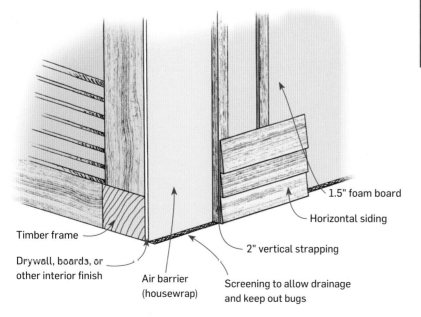

Timber frame

Drywall, boards, or other interior finish

Air barrier (housewrap)

2" vertical strapping

Screening to allow drainage and keep out bugs

Horizontal siding

1.5" foam board

R-Value

R-value is a measure of a building material's resistance to heat flow and is generally used to specify the effectiveness of insulation materials. The R-value for extruded polystyrene foam board is about 5 per inch, while polyisocyanurate foam board is 7 to 8 per inch. Wood such as plywood or siding is about 1 per inch. While the building code may require R-25 or above in the walls of a typical house, this is unnecessary in a small building that you may be heating with an oversized appliance (like a woodstove). It's possible, though, to heat our small building with just the electric lights, given a high enough insulation level.

C. R-15 INSULATION, VERTICAL SIDING

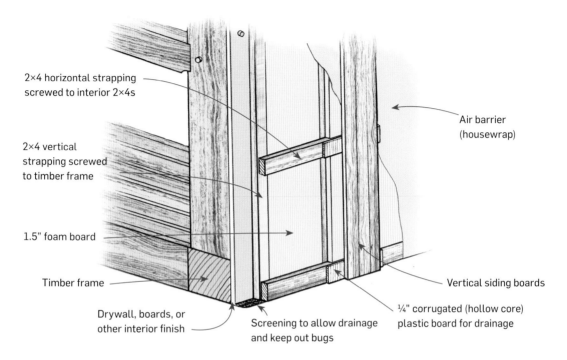

2×4 horizontal strapping
screwed to interior 2×4s

Air barrier
(housewrap)

2×4 vertical
strapping screwed
to timber frame

1.5" foam board

Timber frame

Vertical siding boards

Drywall, boards, or
other interior finish

Screening to allow drainage
and keep out bugs

¼" corrugated (hollow core)
plastic board for drainage

D. NO INSULATION, VERTICAL SIDING

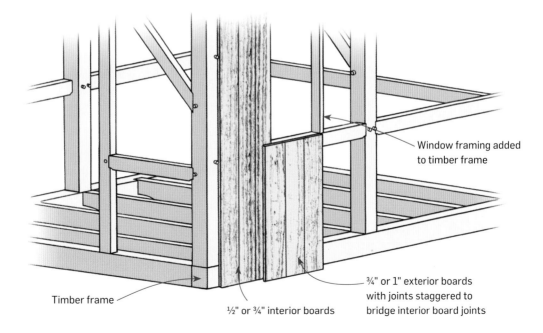

Window framing added
to timber frame

Timber frame

½" or ¾" interior boards

¾" or 1" exterior boards
with joints staggered to
bridge interior board joints

SIPS

The walls and roofs of most modern timber-framed homes are insulated with structural insulated panels (SIPs), which are a sandwich of foam and plywood or oriented strandboard (OSB). SIPs come in a range of thicknesses and are secured to the frame with long screws. On the walls, these panels are shimmed out with ⅝-inch plywood strips on the outside of the timbers. After the SIPs are installed, ½-inch drywall can be slid behind the timbers and screwed to the inside face of the SIPs. On the roof, the drywall is usually painted and laid down over the rafters before the SIPs are installed — plan to do this during dry weather!

SIPs can cost between $5 and $10 per square foot of panel, depending on thickness and manufacturing options (pre-cutting, installation of lumber at edges, electrical chases, etc). The skills to install them are within the grasp of most people, but they can be heavy — about one pound per square foot per inch of thickness — and lifting them up to a roof can be daunting. The most critical step in installation is the sealing of panel joints with spray foam; a continuous seal is essential, since any gap will concentrate

STRUCTURAL INSULATED PANEL (SIP)

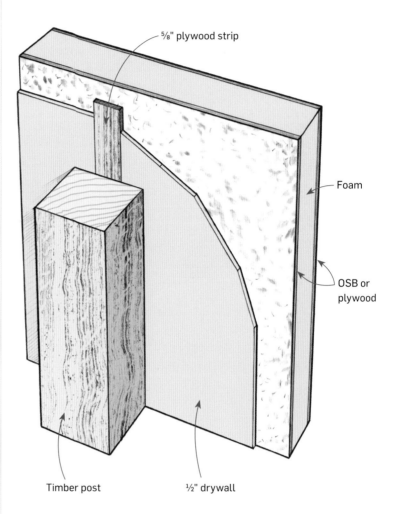

⅝" plywood strip

Foam

OSB or plywood

Timber post

½" drywall

heat loss and condensation in one area and may cause rot.

SIPs save a tremendous amount of labor, since little additional framing is needed, and siding and interior finishes can be screwed or nailed directly to the panel surfaces. However, the materials are more expensive than building up your own wrap-and-strap system, and the economy of labor is not such a big issue on a small building. One sensible compromise might be to use SIPs on the roof where there are few openings (and which you need to get enclosed and insulated quickly), and then do wrap and strap on the walls. However, you may not find it cost-effective to order just a few SIPs for the roof, or even for a very small building. Also, a few specialized tools are needed for cutting and routing panel edges. You can rent these tools, or avoid this task by getting the panels precut, including door and window openings. Precutting does add expense, though, and eliminates the possibility of changing door and window locations during construction.

Most SIP manufacturers provide helpful manuals showing installation details and how to accommodate windows and doors.

INSULATING THE FLOOR

The floor can be insulated between the joists before putting the subflooring down. Nail some strips to the sides of the joists that will support a plywood soffit you can drop in and cover with insulation. If you are building on piers, be sure to cut this soffit accurately and secure it with screws to the strip to keep rodents out; you could also use cementboard or hardware cloth for additional protection. Another option is to lay 1½-inch-thick rigid foam insulation between 2×4 sleepers on top of the subfloor and under the finished flooring, but then you lose headroom and need to adjust the door.

STRUCTURAL INSULATED PANELS (SIPS) *come in various thicknesses and provide a tight insulated envelope on the outside of the timber frame. They are usually pre-cut to fit, installed with a crane, and attached with long screws.*

EPILOGUE

Once you are snug and warm in your finished tiny timber frame, looking up and enjoying your handiwork and the beauty of the wood, we hope you'll appreciate as well the long tradition of the craft you are now a part of. You are also being resourceful and responsible, building small and adding later if need be, and using local materials.

Our philosophy at Heartwood, one that we share with the owners of the buildings you see in this book, can be summed up as follows:

We wish to empower our hands, to train our eyes for quality and beauty in the design of things, and to explore the ways we might live in a more honest relationship with our planet. We believe that a human-scale society can grow amidst the excesses of the old. We share a clear determination to become active creators of our environment as designers and builders and claim back our right to build places that express our care for the life that will happen within them.

It is the same spirit expressed by the poet Gary Snyder when he advised in his book *Turtle Island,*

Find your place on the planet and dig in.

Glossary

adze A handled edged tool with its edge at a right angle to the handle, used to shape or dress timbers.

anisotropic Having a physical property that has a different value when measured in different directions. A simple example is wood, which is stronger along the grain than across it.

arris The edge along which two adjacent surfaces of a timber meet.

bareface tenon A tenon flanked by only one shoulder.

bay The space between two bents; the area between structural cross frames.

beam Any substantial horizontal member in a building's frame.

bent An assembly of timbers perpendicular to the ridge; usually the cross frame of a building, sometimes including rafters, assembled on the ground and then reared up into position.

board foot A volume of wood equalling a piece 12 inches square by 1 inch thick.

boards Wood members 1 inch or less in thickness.

bow Deviation from straight in the length of a timber in the horizontal direction. Also called *sweep*. If the deviation is vertical, it is called **crown**.

boxed heart timber Timber that includes the heart of the tree. Since checks will not cross the heart, such a timber can never split completely.

brace Any diagonal timber (permanent or temporary) that resists distortion of a frame.

bridle An open mortise-and-tenon end joint, such as at a rafter peak or sill corner, with one end of the mortise open; also *tongue-and-fork*.

butt joint An abutment of two timbers without penetration, kept in place by gravity or other timbers, or by ironwork.

cant A block of wood remaining after the better-quality pieces have been cut off.

chamfer A bevel cut at the long arris of a timber, which may be run right through or decoratively stopped before the ends; a bevel at the leading arrises of a tenon, to ease assembly.

check A split that occurs from drying, usually originating from the pith and exiting to the nearest face; not a structural issue in most cases.

cheek The broad surface of a tenon; the corresponding surface of a mortise. The tenon shoulder is usually square to its cheek.

collar The horizontal member fitted between a pair of opposed rafters, used, depending upon position, to prevent sagging or spreading of the rafters.

commander A large wooden mallet typically weighing 10 to 20 pounds; also called a *beetle* or *persuader*.

compression The state of stress in which particles of material tend to be pushed together.

control point Points on a timber from and to which dimensions are laid out.

crown Curvature in a timber's length, placed upward in spanning members where the load will tend to straighten it.

dead load Weight of a building (roof, floors, walls, etc.).

deflection Movement of a structure under a load.

diminished housing A housing with a sloping shoulder to minimize material taken out of the mortised member.

drawbore The traditional fastening technique in which the pin hole in the tenon is deliberately offset from the pin hole in the mortise to draw a joint tight when assembled and fastened with a tapered pin. The proper offset varies with species and scale.

eaves The drip edge of a roof, often overhanging the wall.

FOHC Free of heart center. Timber sawn to exclude the heart can, in theory, be seasoned without checking.

gable roof A double-sloping roof that forms an inverted V.

girt A horizontal timber joining wall posts at a level somewhere between sill and plate. A wall girt runs parallel to the ridge, a bent girt perpendicular; either can support the edge of a floor frame.

grain The pattern of growth rings, rays, and other structural elements in wood made visible by conversion from the tree.

green wood Wood freshly cut, not dried or seasoned.

hardwood Wood of certain deciduous trees, e.g., oak, beech, ash, and the like.

header A wall member bridging the opening for a door or window.

horizontal shear Shear along the grain resulting when a beam is loaded in bending.

housing A shallow mortise or cavity to receive the full section of a timber end for load-bearing; often, but not always, combined with a standard mortise to add bearing area and secure the connection via the tenon.

joinery The work of connecting timbers using woodwork joints; also, the joints themselves.

joist A relatively small timber, usually spaced regularly in sets to support a floor or ceiling.

kerf The slot made by a saw cut.

layout The drawing of a joint on a timber before it is cut; also, the arrangement of timbers into a predetermined pattern for marking.

level Horizontal; parallel to the ground; also, the tool used to check for level or **plumb**.

live load All load other than the permanent weight of a structure, including people, furnishings, snow, wind, earthquake, etc.

loads Forces imposed on a structure.

lumber Wood members 2 inches to 4 inches (nominally) in their smaller dimension.

mapping Layout system wherein joinery in one timber is transferred to another by recording any variations remotely.

mill rule Layout system using timbers that are milled to exact dimensions and are perfectly square.

modulus of elasticity A measure of stiffness of a material; the ratio of stress (force per unit area) to strain (deformation).

mortise The rectangular cavity into which a tenon is inserted.

nominal size Dimensions of a sawn or hewn timber before final sizing; also, what the timber is called (5×7, 8×10, etc.); actual dimensions may be larger or smaller than nominal.

parbuckling Using a loop of rope arranged like a sling for mechanical advantage to raise plates to the tops of posts.

pier A solid support in a foundation system designed to take a vertical load.

pin A short shaft of tough hardwood, often tapered, used to draw together and fasten the traditional mortise-and-tenon joint in timber framing; also called a *peg* or a *trunnel.*

pith The center of the stem of a tree.

plate In normal position, the most important longitudinal timber in a frame. It ties the bents together at their tops and simultaneously stiffens and connects the wall and roof planes while providing a base for the rafters.

plumb Vertical; perpendicular to the ground.

post A vertical or upright supporting timber.

post-and-beam Any structural system made up primarily of vertical and horizontal members.

rafter In a roof frame, any inclined member spanning any part of the distance from eave to peak.

reduction The diminishing of the cross-sectional area of a tenoned member where it goes into a housing.

reference face On a timber to be laid out, the primary surface (which typically receives flooring or wall and roof sheathing) that measurements are taken from. Generally, each timber has two reference surfaces that are adjacent and square to each other. Sometimes called *layout face.*

relish In the case of a mortise cut quite near the end of a timber, material the width and depth of the mortise remaining between the mortise end and the end of the timber; in a tenon, material between the pin hole and the end of the tenon equal in cross-section to the path of the pin through the tenon.

roof pitch Inclination of a roof to the horizontal, usually expressed as inches of rise per 12 inches (1 foot) of run.

scantlings A set of standard dimensions for parts of a structure; also, the size to which a piece of wood or stone is measured and cut.

scarf To join two equal-section timbers in their length to make a longer beam; also, the joint so used.

scribe rule General term for layout systems in which each timber is custom-mated to its neighbors. The process requires setting out all the timbers for a given assembly in a framing yard or on a floor, positioned relatively as they will ultimately rest in the building. Variations are transferred between timbers directly.

shear The state of stress wherein particles of material tend to slide relative to one another; also, the force inducing such stress. Vertical (cross-grain) shear loads also impart horizontal (long-grain) shear stress.

sheathing A covering of rough boards or sheet goods on exterior walls or roofs, usually itself covered by an additional weatherproof layer of material.

shoulder In a mortise-and-tenon joint, the element of the tenoned member that is perpendicular to the tenon cheek, and which lies against the face of the mortised member; there can be as few as one and as many as four shoulders on the tenoned member.

shrinkage Reduction in section and length of a timber as it dries.

SIP (structural insulated panel) A sandwich of two layers of sheet goods enclosing and bonded to a core of thermal insulation.

sill A horizontal timber that rests upon the foundation and links the posts in a frame.

sizing Planing hewn or rough-sawn timber to uniform section, by hand locally at the joints, or by machine for the whole timber.

sleepers Large-sectioned timbers placed on the ground to support stacks of timber.

soffit tenon A horizontal tenon with its lower cheek coplanar with the lower surface of the timber.

softwood The wood of conifers or evergreens, e.g., pine, spruce, Douglas fir, and the like.

span In a roof frame, the horizontal distance covered by a rafter; in a beam, the unsupported distance between two neighboring posts or other support members.

spokeshave An extremely short plane with wing handles in line with the edge of the blade. Pushed or pulled, it is used for forming and finishing curved surfaces.

square At an angle of 90 degrees; also, a measuring tool so angled.

square rule Layout system in which a smaller, perfect timber is envisioned within a rough outer timber; joints are cut to this inner timber. Many timbers in a square-rule frame are interchangeable.

stick frame A frame built with lumber pieces spaced relatively close together and simple connections joined with nails.

stickers Spacers used between stacked timbers or boards to provide air circulation.

stub tenon An abbreviated unpinned tenon designed for locating a timber (usually the bottom of a post) into a shallow mortise during raising.

stud A minor vertical member in a framed wall or partition, usually used only as a nailer for wall coverings.

subflooring A covering of rough boards or sheet goods that goes on top of joists and below finished flooring.

table The broad surface of a housing.

taper A gradual reduction of the cross-section of a tenon, timber, or pin.

template A full-size pattern of thin material, used for laying out and checking joints and for other purposes.

tenon A rectangular projection resulting from cutting into the end of a timber, flanked by one or more resulting **shoulders** and sized to match a mating **mortise**.

tension The state of stress in which particles of material tend to be pulled apart.

through tenon A tenon that passes right through the timber it joins; it may be cut off flush, or it may extend past the outside face of the mortised member to be wedged or locked in place by one of several means.

tie beam An important horizontal transverse frame member that resists the tendency of the roof to push the walls outward. The tie beam may be found at the top of the walls, where it is able to receive the thrust of the rafters directly, or it may be found as much as several feet lower down the walls, where it joins principal posts in tension connections.

timber A large (5 inches or greater in its smallest dimension) squared or dressed piece of wood ready for fashioning as one member of a structure.

timber frame A frame of large timbers connected by structural woodwork joints and supporting small timbers to which roof, walls, and floors are fastened.

twist Deviation from plane in the surface of a timber; also called *wind*.

wetting bush The ceremonial tree branch (of the same species as the frame, ideally) that is nailed to the peak once the roof frame is complete. This symbolically re-establishes the roots of the building for longevity and expresses gratitude to the trees that create the structure.

Comparative Design Values of Common Wood Species Used in Timber Framing

Grade: #2 Beams and Stringers

Fiber stress in bending, or Fb (in psi), is a measure of the strength of the species:

→ Eastern White Pine: 575
→ Douglas Fir: 875
→ Eastern Hemlock: 750
→ Red Oak: 875
→ White Oak: 750
→ White Cedar: 500

Shear parallel to the grain, or Fv (in psi), tells us (for example) how much we can notch the ends of our floor joists:

→ Eastern White Pine: 125
→ Douglas Fir: 170
→ Eastern Hemlock: 155
→ Red Oak: 155
→ White Oak: 205
→ White Cedar: 115

Modulus of elasticity, or E (in psi), tells us the stiffness of the species, which rules the design of floor joists so they don't bounce; it's less of a concern with rafters:

→ Eastern White Pine: 900,000
→ Douglas Fir: 1,300.000
→ Eastern Hemlock: 900,000
→ Red Oak: 1,000,000
→ White Oak: 800,000
→ White Cedar: 600,000

CHISEL SHARPENING

Most edge tools are not truly sharp when you buy them and must be honed and maintained to keep a keen and proper cutting profile. The topic of sharpening is a book unto itself, and everyone has their favorite system; here we'll focus on chisels, since they will get the most daily use. Plane irons can be sharpened in the same manner.

The first step after acquiring a chisel is to make sure that the cutting edge is square to the sides; this can be checked with your combination square. If it's not square, then only part of the cutting edge will get to the bottom of a mortise and sharpening will

Check the angle of the bevel with a bevel gauge and protractor.

be difficult. Also check the angle of the bevel at the front; it should be between 25 and 30 degrees and can be measured with a bevel gauge (sliding T-bevel) and a protractor. If either of these conditions aren't met (common in antique tools), or if there are some serious nicks in the cutting edge, then you should grind the bevel until it is true. This can be done on a stationary wheel grinder or a belt sander, if you are patient and careful not to heat up the metal too much, which destroys the temper in the steel. You could also take the tool to a machinist for this work, but that may cost more than buying a new chisel.

Once the bevel is set, then you are ready to sharpen (a grinder or belt sander alone will not give you a good enough edge). There are numerous choices and prices for sharpening stones, and advantages to each:

→ Oil stones are the least expensive and very durable, but they are messy and slow and can't be flattened once they wear out.

→ Waterstones (natural or synthetic) are very affordable but need to be flattened regularly, as they wear quickly. They sharpen tools fast and give the best results, in my opinion.

→ Ceramic waterstones are so durable they can last a lifetime. They come in extremely fine grits and are comparatively expensive.

→ Diamond stones stay flat, can be used wet or dry, and are the most expensive, although you can buy one stone with different grits on each side.

There are two other options worth mentioning. Wet/dry sandpaper adhered to a flat piece of reinforced glass or stone works well, but will end up being the most expensive option over time. If you do a lot of sharpening, you may want to purchase an electric sharpening machine such as the Tormek or Work Sharp.

SHARPENING WITH A STONE

You'll want a stone that is at least 2 inches wide by 8 inches long for chisel and plane iron sharpening. You should have at least two different grits: a medium grit for establishing

Continued on the next page →

the microbevel and a fine grit for finishing. Even finer grits can give you mirrored, razor-sharp edges.

1. The sharpest cutting edge is the intersection between two polished, flat surfaces. This means the back must be flat, so before working the beveled side, "lap" the back of the chisel on a flat stone until you see it hitting along the edges and at least ⅛ inch or so behind the cutting edge. This is the only time you'll work the back of the chisel except to remove any "burr." Do not lift up the handle, or you'll put an undesired bevel on the back side.

2. Turn the chisel over and lay the bevel on the stone, lifting up the handle until you feel the bevel hit the stone or you see a bit of oil or water squirt out from the front edge. Then lift the handle up another inch or so in the back to establish a 1- or 2-degree microbevel that will save you having to sharpen the entire main bevel. Support the chisel as fully as possible with your hands, lock your elbows into your sides, and rock forward and back on your feet while guiding the chisel with

A honing guide can help you hold the correct angle.

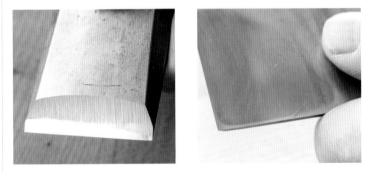

A properly sharpened chisel has a polished microbevel and is flat on the back.

moderate pressure over the entire stone. Some people use a figure-eight motion to wear down the stone as evenly as possible.

3. Once the microbevel is honed, flip the chisel over and draw it back lightly once or twice to remove any burr, keeping it dead-flat on the stone.

There are a variety of honing guides on the market to help you hold the proper angle on the stone. I found most of them too cumbersome to use until I discovered the Veritas Mk.II, which I use all the time and is easy to find online.

To test for sharpness, you can push the chisel along a plastic pen body — if it catches you should be good to go. Numerous websites and videos online can help you out if you need more guidance. And practice, practice, practice.

Resources

ORGANIZATIONS

The Heartwood School for the Homebuilding Crafts
Washington, Massachusetts
413-623-6677
heartwoodschool.com

Northeastern Lumber Manufacturers Association (NeLMA)
Cumberland Center, Maine
207-829-6901
nelma.org

Publishes Standard Grading Rules for Northeastern Lumber, which includes structural design values for many Northeastern softwood and hardwood species

Structural Insulated Panel Association (SIPA)
Fort Lauderdale, Florida
253-858-7472
sips.org

Information on SIPs (including construction details) and contact information for suppliers

Timber Framers Guild
855-598-1803
tfguild.org

Nonprofit organization dedicated to preserving the craft of timber framing

The Guild also includes:
- *The Timber Frame Business Council, a special interest group that provides resources and links to suppliers, including for tools, timber, and hardware*
- *The Timber Frame Engineering Council, which publishes technical bulletins and provides contact information for structural engineers specializing in timber framing*
- *The Traditional Timberframe Research and Advisory Group (TTRAG), which specializes in historic timber-framed structures*

ONLINE FORUMS

The Forestry Forum
forestryforum.com

Timber Framers Guild
forums.tfguild.net

PINS

Northcott Wood Turning
Walpole, New Hampshire
603-756-4204
pegs.us

TO FIND A SAWMILL NEAR YOU

Forestry Forum Services Database
forestryforum.com/datasearch.html

Portable Sawmill Finder
portablesawmill.info

You may also find directories of sawmills by doing a general online search with your state or province name and "lumber producers" or "wood processors."

Wood-Mizer Pro Sawyer Network
woodmizer.com

TOOL SUPPLIERS

New timber framing tools are not hard to find if you search online. Here are some suppliers we particularly recommend:

Jim Bode Tools
Elizaville, New York
518-537-8665
jimbodetools.com
Refurbished antique hand tools for timber framing

The Superior Works
Patrick Leach
Ashby, Massachusetts
leach@supertool.com
supertool.com
Antique hand tools for timber framing

Timberwolf Tools
Newry, Maine
800-869-4169
timberwolftools.com
Power tools for timber framing

Timber Framers Guild
855-598-1803
tfguild.org
Supplier of Borneman Layout Template

Timber Tools
Niagara Falls, New York
800-350-8176
timbertools.com
Hand and power tools for timber framing and log building

Barr Specialty Tools
McCall, Idaho
800-235-4452
barrtools.com
Chisels, adzes, mallets and other hand-forged tools for timber framing

Vintage Tools NE
Jim Rogers Sawmill
Georgetown, Massachusetts
978-352-2735
jrsawmill.com/Timber_Framing_Tools_For_Sale.htm
Refurbished antique hand tools for timber framing

Timber Frame Headquarters
Brice Cochran
Mountain Rest, South Carolina
888-552-9379
timberframehq.com
Plans, books, and tools

Lee Valley & Veritas Tools
leevalley.com
800-871-8158
Timber framing hand tools, Veritas Mk.II honing guide

Bibliography

Benson, Tedd. *The Timber-Frame Home*, rev. ed. Taunton Press, 1997.
  Good book on timber frame design and related systems, such as foundations, enclosures, plumbing, electric, etc.

Chappell, Steve. *A Timber Framer's Workshop*. Fox Maple Press, 2011.
  Design, engineering, and wood technology as applied to timber framing

Rower, Ken, ed. *Timber Framing Fundamentals*. Timber Framers Guild, 2011.
  Numerous articles from the quarterly journal Timber Framing *for those new to the craft; subjects include layout (including scribe rule), tools, design, engineering, raising, and rigging.*

Sobon, Jack A. *Build a Classic Timber-Framed House*. Storey Publishing, 1994.
  Best book for a supplemental reference on square rule layout and for the projects in this book

——. *Historic American Timber Joinery*. Timber Framers Guild, 2002.
  Graphic catalogue of joints, including those used in projects here

Sobon, Jack A., and Roger Schroeder. *Timber Frame Construction*. Storey Publishing, 1984.
  Original version of our core timber frame with more square rule procedures

Timber Framers Guild. *Timber Framing*, the quarterly journal of the Timber Framers Guild, 1985–2014.
  Index, CD of back issues, and individual copies available

Index

Page numbers in *italics* indicate illustrations and photographs.
Page numbers in **bold** font indicate charts and tables.

KEEP BUILDING WITH THESE STOREY BOOKS

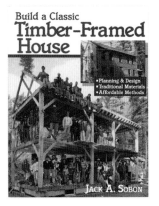

by Jack A. Sobon

With these step-by-step instructions, you can build your own enduring, affordable, classic timber-framed house. Architect and author Jack Sobon covers everything from finding the right building site, selecting the best timber, using economical hand tools, and much more.

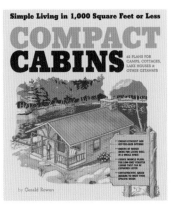

by Gerald Rowan

Simple living in 1,000 square feet or less — with 62 design interpretations for every taste, this fully illustrated guide will inspire your dream cabin. These innovative floor plans are flexible, with modular elements to mix and match.

by Brett McLeod

Make the most of your forest with this comprehensive manual to homesteading. Author and forest professor Brett McLeod will teach you how to raise livestock, harvest firewood and building supplies, grow food, and more on your own woodland.

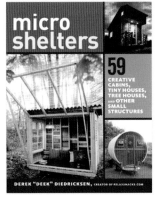

by Derek "Deek" Diedricksen

Get inspired with this gorgeous collection of creative and inspiring cabins, forts, studios, and other microshelters — including full-color photos, floor plans, building guidelines, and more.

These and other books from Storey Publishing are available wherever quality books are sold or by calling 1-800-441-5700. Visit us at www.storey.com or sign up for our newsletter at www.storey.com/signup.